PRAISE FOR
PREACHING STICKY SERMONS

"We can all use a little help in the area of preaching. That's one reason I'm a big fan of RookiePreacher.com and why I love that Brandon and Joe have put together a book of both the spiritual and the practical. I mean, college and seminary are great for some things, but I'm guessing no one talked about how to handle criticisms of your sermons in social media, right? Or using Evernote and Google Docs to stay organized and shave hours off your prep time? *Preaching Sticky Sermons* is a great addition to your toolbox as you share the most important message the world will ever hear. This is a manual for preaching in the trenches."

– Tim Harlow, senior pastor of Parkview Christian Church and author of *Life on Mission*

"Where was this book when I started preaching twenty years ago? We all know there's a lot of material, advice, and helpful tips in regards to sermon writing available on the web or on your bookshelves, the issue is the time it takes to find it. This book has everything you need in regards to sermon writing gathered at your fingertips.

What you will love about this book is that it's a one-stop, go-to manual for sermon writing. *Preaching Sticky Sermons* is filled with practical sermon writing tips; time management ideas and other insights that will help you write a memorable or "sticky" sermon each and every week. It's a book that will be highlighted and dog-eared as you return to it time and time again. *Preaching Sticky Sermons* will be a book that you will keep with you along with your Bible, notebook, laptop, or whatever you use to craft and write your sermons. Thanks Brandon and Joe for making the weekly sermon writing process simpler and stickier!"

– Kenny White, lead pastor of The Crossing Church

"It has been a pleasure watching Brandon Kelly and Joe Hoagland grow their platform for helping preachers get better. Their *Rookie Preacher* website is a constant source of quality content which is helping pastors more effectively steward the most important message in human history, the life-changing message of Jesus Christ. If you enjoy their website, then you'll love their book *Preaching Sticky Sermons*. Brandon and Joe are gifts to the body of Christ. This book proves it and those who listen to you each Sunday will be grateful you read it."

– Brian Dodd, author of *The 10 Indispensable Practices of the 2-Minute Leader*, blogger, and director of new ministry relationships of Injoy Stewardship Solutions

"I love preaching the Scriptures. Period. I consider it a calling from God, one I don't take lightly. A call to preach is a call to preparation. A prepared preacher is a powerful preacher. This is the reason I am excited about *Preaching Sticky Sermons*. Brandon Kelley and Joe Hoagland have unearthed homiletical flint to sharpen the tools of aspiring and seasoned preachers. *Preaching Sticky Sermons* is practical, challenging, innovative, and filled with a treasure trove of preaching wisdom. Each section is a sort of practical lecture and lab, where the preacher can learn from, not ivory tower theoreticians, but humble practitioners. Though I have been preaching for over twenty years, I am excited to use this book as my bible for preaching sticky sermons."

– Marvin Williams, lead pastor of Trinity Church, Lansing, Michigan and author at Our Daily Bread Ministries

"Good preaching is an art form and often a messy process. God has used the preaching of His word for centuries to convey His love for His people and to grow their faith. I love how *Preaching Sticky Sermons* stays practical while allowing for individual preachers to maintain their voice and let the Holy Spirit speak through them. Each section clearly communicates a unique aspect of preaching making this book a manual of sorts that I think you'll be referencing over and over again. This resource is timely and needed in today's Church!"

– Jonathan Pearson, author of *Next Up: 8 Shifts Great Young Leaders Make*, pastor, podcaster, and blogger at JonathanPearson.net

PREACHING STICKY SERMONS

A Practical Guide to Preparing, Writing, and Delivering Memorable Sermons

Brandon Kelley and Joe Hoagland

Preaching Sticky Sermons:
*A Practical Guide to Preparing, Writing, and
Delivering Memorable Sermons*

© 2016 by Brandon Kelley and Joe Hoagland
All rights reserved.

Published by Rainer Publishing
www.RainerPublishing.com

ISBN 978-0-9978861-5-3

Printed in the United States of America

Scripture quotations are from the ESV ® Bible
(The Holy Bible, English Standard Version ®),
copyright © 2001 by Crossway, a publishing ministry of Good
News Publishers. Used by permission. All rights reserved.

Table of Contents

Foreword 11
Introduction 15
Section 1: Great Preaching Begins With Great Preparation 19
1: Prepare Yourself First 21
2: The Transformative Principle for Your Sermon Prep 23
3: Sample Sermon Prep Processes 27
4: Prepare Your Sermon in Ten Minutes (for Practice) 33
5: Keys for Great Exegesis 37
6: Get the Right Tools 43
7: How to Take Evernote to the Next Level 49
8: Sermon Series Planning 55
9: Planning a Year of Preaching 63
Section 2: Write For Maximum Impact 67
10: When You're Not Feeling Creative 69
11: Topical Preaching? 73
12: Expository Preaching? 77
13: A Better Sermon Type 81
14: Best Practices for Outlining 85
15: Structuring a Sticky Sermon 89

- 16: Reasons You Should Manuscript Your Message ... 95
- 17: How to Move From Manuscript to Preaching Notes 99
- 18: How to Create an Engaging Introduction 103
- 19: Identify and Expose the Tension 107
- 20: Timeless Truth, Timely Application 113
- 21: Target the Heart...117
- 22: Keys to Closing Your Sermon Powerfully 123
- 23: Life-Changing Calls to Action................................... 127
- 24: Using Illustrations..135
- 25: Weaving a Single Story Throughout Your Sermon 141

Section 3: Deliver Intentionally and Powerfully 145
- 26: What to Do When You're Done Writing Your sermon... 147
- 27: Do You Get Nervous Before Preaching?..................151
- 28: One Powerful Characteristic of Great Preaching 155
- 29: How to Get Rid of Filler Words.................................161
- 30: Focus Your Focus..165
- 31: Move to Move Hearts...169
- 32: Capture the Emotion of the Text 173
- 33: Your Vocal Toolbox... 179
- 34: Repetition and Emphasis 183
- 35: What You Need to Know About Using Media 185

Section 4: Beyond Sunday...189
- 36: Evaluate Your Last Sermon 191
- 37: How to Take Your Sermon Past Sunday 195

38: How to Handle Bad Sermon Criticism....................199
39: Fellowship With Area Preachers............................203
Conclusion.. 207

Foreword

When people ask me how I lasted through the early days of transitioning a nearly dead, 40-year-old church, my answer is consistent, top-notch preaching.

Even those who aren't with you, have a harder time hating you when you are feeding them.

The worship wars of the 80s and 90s created some unforgettable split personalities within churches. None of these were more dramatic than the worship battle I walked into as a new pastor at a tiny church in Tinley Park, IL.

It was in the early 90s—the throes of the worship wars. We had a unique situation in that you got both sides depending on which week you were there. One week a bearded, longhaired mailman got up and played "praise" songs in his full hippie glory. The next week a suit-and-tie guy would stand up and lead the congregation in hymns. He was convinced that if *every verse* of every hymn wasn't sung, some of the theology would be lost and the building would burn down. Or something. So if you invited someone to church, you never knew if you were getting Woodstock or the Mormon Tabernacle Choir.

We were also struggling over the role of women

and many other issues. The church was on life support. There were no elders left; they had either quit or been chased away by the other side. The church was being held together by our local church planting organization (who was probably hoping the thing would just die so they could sell the building and plant something effective).

As a 28-year-old lead pastor, for the first time in my life I was supposed to negotiate a truce to this civil war.

Needless to say, no matter what I did, some people were going to be upset. For *years* people were mad at me. After seven years we took a vote to move the church because we were out of parking and couldn't grow, and 44 percent of the congregation still voted against it.

But here's the secret. It's hard for people to stay mad at you when you're baptizing their neighbors and introducing their friends to Jesus.

As a pastor, you can make a lot of mistakes and still grow a church. But one thing you can't afford to let go is the preaching of the Word. A church just won't grow without solid, compelling preaching.

And we can all use a little help in that area. That's one reason I'm a big fan of RookiePreacher.com, and why I love that Brandon and Joe have put together a book of both the spiritual and the practical. I mean, college and seminary are great for some things, but I'm guessing no one talked about how to handle criticisms of your sermons in social media, right? Or using Evernote and Google Docs to stay organized and shave hours off your prep time? *Preaching Sticky Sermons* is a great addition to your toolbox as you share the most important message the world will ever hear.

This is a manual for preaching in the trenches.

Praying for you,

– Tim Harlow, senior pastor of Parkview Christian Church and author of *Life on Mission*

Introduction

Every Sunday millions of people gather together to worship God and hear his word proclaimed. For many of these church attenders, the preaching is what keeps them coming back. Now, it used to be that public speaking was a regular mode of communication. But as it becomes more and more rare, preachers encounter more and more challenges to connecting through it.

In this book we walk you step by step on how to prepare, write, and deliver life-changing sermons. But first, is preaching still relevant?

Preaching as Christian Numbers Decline

There is a popular study by Pew Research that illustrates the declining numbers Americans who identify with Christianity today.

Of course this will concern many people, and many will also celebrate these findings. But what does this mean for preaching?

As with this so-called decline of Christianity, there is also a so-called decline in preaching. It's irrelevant, it's boring, and it serves no purpose anymore.

Preaching remains relevant even as America pushes more post-Christian for at least three reasons.

Preaching Proclaims God's Word
No matter how much the raw numbers of Christianity decline, Christian preaching will still be relevant because it proclaims God's Word. Preaching rooted in the Bible will always reveal truth no matter if it is the first century or the twenty-first century. The Bible will always be relevant because God is always relevant.

Preaching Speaks Truth into Lives
Preaching is able to take the truths rooted in Scripture and apply them to modern life. For this reason, it is still vitally important. Preaching provides modern application of the Bible and helps people learn about God and the teachings of his people in a way that can be understood.

Preaching is Ever Evolving in Style
Preaching is not the same as it was in Jesus's and the Apostle Paul's time. It's not the same as the early church or the medieval church or even when the likes of Jonathan Edwards gained a following. That is because preaching style can change with the appetite of the popular culture. It can incorporate media or audience interaction or other innovations that make it more palatable for evolving culture.

INTRODUCTION

No End in Sight
Even though many people are calling for the end of Christianity, the end of God in America, and by extension the end of preaching, it remains a vital practice in the lives of many. Millions of people hear God's truth proclaimed through a preached message on Sunday morning or Saturday night or another day every week throughout the year.

WHY WE WROTE THIS BOOK

We both went to Bible college and had our fair share of preaching classes that assigned many different preaching books. Many of these were valuable and insightful; however, we often walked away with unanswered questions.

One big catalyst for putting together this resource is our website RookiePreacher.com where we help pastors preach and lead better. We found that the practical approach we were taking to preaching was resonating with pastors all over the world.

We wanted to put together a practical and accessible resource for preachers young, old, and everything in between. We believe this is a fresh take on preaching in the twenty-first century.

HOW THIS BOOK IS ORGANIZED

We designed this book to be an easy-to-use reference that preachers can revisit throughout their ministry. To make this as practical as possible, there are thirty-nine chapters that all focus on different aspects of preaching. So if you need to reference something specific, you can find where it is in the table of contents without having to wade through long pieces of text.

You'll notice four different sections. Section one focuses on preparation so that you can prepare your best sermons. Section two is all about the specifics of writing each part of your sermon so that it is as effective as it can be. Section three is designed to help you intentionally deliver your sermon in the most impactful way possible. Section four is going to help you go past Sunday in your work as a preacher.

Our Prayer For You

We pray that this resource helps you prepare, write, and deliver sermons more confidently and that more people would experience life-change as they respond to the messages you preach.

Thank you for giving us the opportunity to walk on this journey with you.

Section 1: Great Preaching Begins With Great Preparation

1: PREPARE YOURSELF FIRST

We are going to talk a lot in this book about preparing sermons. Many other people and books do the same. It's an important process in one of the most important weekly rituals that takes place in the world today.

But other resources sometimes neglect the actual process before you begin to formally prepare the sermon. This is the process of preparing yourself to prepare a sermon.

There are three major mindsets that I try to embody before I begin the actual sermon preparation process.

Be in the Right Place Spiritually
This involves consistent spiritual discipline, and a root in God's word, When I slack in this area I notice the effects immediately. Whether it is the sermon falling flat with ideas or the sermon not having the impact that it could have, I feel it. The point is that before we start the process of crafting a sermon that communicates God's message to his people we must be in a place with God ourselves that is consistent and thorough.

Be in the Right Place Culturally

This is important and one of the main ways we can connect with culture is by reading and keeping up to date with happenings in the world. But it also requires a sharp eye on events and trends shaping culture. Whether it is to educate your audience on these trends or give a biblical perspective, this is an important discipline.

Be in the Right Place Contextually

Beyond being culturally in the right place, as communicators we must also be contextually in the right place. That is, you must be wholly aware of what does and does not matter or what does and does not communicate in your specific context. I cringe when I see preachers speaking on topics or to ideas that have nothing to do with their context in the name of "relevance" or because of outright unawareness of their context. Much preaching, pastoring, and leading is contextual, and without this discipline all the preparation in the world will fall flat.

2: THE TRANSFORMATIVE PRINCIPLE FOR YOUR SERMON PREP

Once we ourselves are prepared to prepare sermons we can start the preparation process. We have to take many things into account as we prepare sermons. But with those many things there is one key we want to start with: *consistency*. Just like anything in life and leading and preaching, consistency is important. More specifically, we need to seek out consistent routines for ourselves in sermon preparation.

Not that long ago my sermon preparation process was scattered and sporadic because my preaching schedule was sporadic. Before I became the senior pastor at my first church, I preached at most ten times a year. So every time I was called out from the bullpen, so to speak, I would have a blank slate to write and deliver a sermon. There usually would be no sermon series to plug into usually, and definitely not one I had planned. So I would start a week or two in advance and pretty much wing the process, experiment here, try something new there, and so on.

Really though, this was a good experience for me because I was able to see what worked and what didn't. I developed my systems for text study, developing application, and so on.

The Realization

"You need to come up with a consistent routine," I told myself a couple weeks after I started this senior ministry role. When I took over it was on an interim basis, I was in the last month of college, and the church was an hour and a half a way. These factors made me realize I needed to develop a plan for consistency and stick with it. So I developed the plan in the next chapter. Over the course of time I have experimented and tweaked the formula a bit, but overall I've stayed consistent with it, and it has made a tremendous difference.

I strive for consistency. I want a system in place to allow me to develop and craft the sermon no matter what life and ministry throw at me. This has led me to develop goal mileposts throughout the week, which I stick to as best as I possibly can.

Develop Consistency for Yourself

You need develop a plan that you can adhere to consistently. Go through your sermon prep process now. Figure out what you need to accomplish by the end of each workday. Write down this plan and go for it. This week!

You'll be glad when you have developed a consistent process, plan, system, or schedule for your sermon preparation. Believe me. Consistency has helped me a lot.

3: SAMPLE SERMON PREP PROCESSES

It's interesting how many different ways different pastors prepare their sermons. You may be someone who is trying to find a new way to do sermon prep, or you may be someone who is trying to just find *a* way to do sermon prep. This chapter will give you an idea of what both our processes look like.

Brandon's Process

My method has changed fairly frequently. I've experimented with a few different things, as I am always trying to learn a better way. Below is what I have found works best. In every step, I approach this process in an attitude and posture of prayer. My biggest prayer is that God will push me to the side and that he would take over and simply use me as a tool to accomplish what he would like to do. That is my prayer in sermon prep as well as right before I go up to preach on Sunday.

Monday

I start the week off by looking at the text I will be preaching. I'll begin praying and seeking what God is saying through this text and what he desires to be preached on Sunday. I don't research on Monday; instead, I simply let the text itself simmer. As the day goes on, I'm thinking about the text and about life. Many times I'll have developed an illustration or angle for approaching the text by the end of the day.

Tuesday

Tuesday is research day for me. I open back up to the text that I am preaching and begin to take notes on each verse. Once I've done this and have understood the flow of the text, I begin looking at other people's thoughts on it. I'll look at commentaries in my physical library, in my Kindle library, and on the Internet that I find through a few Bible study websites.

Once I have taken notes from commentaries and my own textual study, I compile them into Evernote so they are in one, easily accessible place. If I don't already have some illustrations or stories in mind, I'll begin to think through what I've experienced that relates to the text. I also think through things I've discovered in books, articles, and podcasts.

Wednesday

At this point, my attention turns to determining the main point, or bottom line, of the message. This is not an easy task, so don't write it off. I think through the entire text and entire message I will be preaching and boil it down to one memorable statement that people can take with them for, hopefully, a long time.

Once I have the bottom line, I begin outlining my message on a white board and in Google Docs. In the next section I'll show you how I structure my sermons, which impacts how I outline them in the preparation process.

When I have the outline finished, I begin writing out my message in full manuscript form (word for word).

Thursday

Many times I don't finish the manuscript writing process on Wednesday, so I'll complete it first thing on Thursday. After this I boil the message down from manuscript form to what I will preach from.

Next is something that, surprisingly, many preachers don't do—I go through the message verbally. By the end of the prep week, I want to have gone through the message a total of six times—three with the manuscript and three with the preaching notes. I don't always get to six, but I make it a point to get close.

Friday

At this point, all that is left is to go through the message a couple more times (depending on how the week went), send my notes to the tech team, and then create message slides. As far as slides go, I keep it simple. They consist of the Scripture and my bottom line. Rarely will they include something more (pictures, graphs, etc.).

Sunday
Preach!

Joe's Process

My process is pretty consistent from week to week. On Monday and Tuesday, I am mainly looking for the context of the passage or topic that I am preaching with commentaries and other sermons. I then start compiling potential illustrations. On Wednesday I put it all together, and on Thursday I work on exactly how I want to present the sermon text I have. I segment a specific portion of time on Saturday night for prayer specific to the sermon and people who are going to hear.

Monday

I begin the week by finding the text I'll be preaching and study it.

Tuesday

I'll continue studying the text and also bring in some other resources. These consist of commentaries and past sermons. Once I've done this and know where my message is going, I'll begin to compile illustration ideas.

Wednesday

This is the day where most everything comes together. This is a big part of the process. As I have gone along on Monday and Tuesday I have compiled everything into a "preachable" Google Doc. This is something that I could take up front with me and preach from. This has an introduction, conclusion, application, transitions, main sub points, and so on.

Thursday

On Thursday I take a long look at the Google Doc I have and then adapt that into what comes into the pulpit with me on Sunday.

4: PREPARE YOUR SERMON IN TEN MINUTES (FOR PRACTICE)

Now that you have seen our weeklong, drawn-out preparation processes, we are going to shock your system a little bit.

What if I told you that you could actually prepare a sermon in ten minutes instead of ten hours? Would you believe me? Would you write it off as resulting in a terrible message with no substance? I'm sure you are skeptical, but just go with me. I'm always looking for ways to improve as a preacher. One thing I've started doing is preparing a message in ten minutes every week. And not only do I prepare it, but I also deliver it. Every week—ten minutes of sermon prep. And I believe this is making me become a better preacher.

Before you freak out, I am not talking about the Sunday morning sermon. I prepare and deliver this message every week on my podcast. Now, I want to make this clear: you don't have to have a podcast in order to take advantage of this way to improve. In fact, you don't even have to do it every week. Do it once a month, twice a month, whatever you want.

This Will Make You a Better Preacher

The purpose behind taking only ten minutes to prepare a sermon is to stretch yourself. Every week you preach, I'm sure you spend hours upon hours on sermon preparation. And this isn't a bad thing. But preparing a message in ten minutes forces you to simplify your message. You end up thinking of ideas rather than full-fledged paragraphs. You force your brain to get on its toes.

When you force yourself to create an engaging and impactful message in such a little amount of time, you'll find that once you map out your next sermon for Sunday you'll have a much easier time thinking of illustrations, applications, and the overall flow of the message.

Preparing a sermon in ten minutes will force you to have a *rhyme to your sermon prep reason*. You'll be forced to come up with a consistent structure to your message that you'll generally follow. I've fleshed out the way I create engaging messages that are purpose filled and action driven. For the sake of my ten-minute sermon prep, I use the method you'll see in the next section.

Once you get to the point of delivering this message, you'll want to let it go and start preaching. If you are used to writing a manuscript for your message and depending on those notes throughout your delivery, you'll find that this is going to be a stretch. But I think it'll be a good stretch.

PREPARE YOUR SERMON IN TEN MINUTES (FOR PRACTICE)

How to Do It
1. Read and understand the text you are preaching.
2. Decide what your one point will be.
3. Ask yourself how this passage goes against our assumptions, way of life, actions, etc.
4. Think of a way to engage your audience.
5. Decide how you will build tension in light of #3.
6. Use #2 to flesh out a practical application and action step.
7. Determine what is at state if listeners don't take heed to the application and inspiration? Use this to build some sort of inspiration at the end.
8. Write down a word or phrase under each heading.
9. Preach it! (I keep my message to fifteen minutes when I do this.)

This Is about Practice
I am not advocating that you throw out your weekly sermon preparation process. What I *am* advocating is that you stretch yourself in a different venue, whether that be delivering this sermon in a podcast or simply to yourself. I've decided to do this every week, but that doesn't mean you have to. Just decide what will work best for you. I do this on my off day or late at night or early in the morning in the fringe hours of my day.

I believe that preparing a sermon in ten minutes will make you into a better preacher. Will you try it? Just once?

PREACHING STICKY SERMONS

What would it hurt? If you enjoy preaching, you'll find that this way of practicing is a lot of fun!

5: KEYS FOR GREAT EXEGESIS

Every sermon you preach should be focused on God's Word, not your own ideas, opinions, or anecdotes. If you want to see God work in a special way through your message, it must be biblically true. If you have or are attending Bible college or seminary, you've been or are being trained in this. But we would do you a disservice if we talked about the practical elements of preaching without addressing this all-important aspect of preaching–biblical exegesis.

Let's get started.

Follow the Author's Flow–Don't Cut Him Off
Whether you preach expository messages, topical messages, or whatever other type of message you want to call it, it's vital to realize that chapter breaks and section headings are not part of the text; they are later additions. Yes, I know this is quite elementary, and I'm sure you are way past that, but we must realize that these breaks and headings do play a part in how we read the text.

Let's say, for a minute, that you are preaching through a book of the Bible. If you planned your series ahead of time without reading the entire book and following the author's thought flow, recognizing where he transitions to different topics, you'll be tempted to simply break it up by chapter or by half-chapters. Likely, you'll find that there are times (not always) when you regret breaking the text up the way your Bible does.

Choose the better way. Instead of blindly following chapter breaks and section headings, read the text carefully and ignore those two things. Follow the author's thought progression and see where he transitions to something different. This is especially vital in studying the New Testament Epistles because they follow an exhortation structure. For instance, there's a reason Paul explains theological realities before he calls Christians to live a certain way. Could it be that the two are connected? I think so.

Know the Historical Context

There's a reason most Bible colleges and seminaries require Roman history or ancient Near Eastern history as classes for Bible students. This is one of the biggest things your congregation is likely to lack. Yet, when you take the time to understand the historical context of the first century and prior, the picture you arrive to is vibrant and detailed. Without it, you're left with something that is less.

Most commentaries attempt to take into account the historical context of a passage, and many do a good job, but a commentary is no substitute for books focused solely on the historical context of the Bible. This way requires more reading, more work, and more study, but it's completely worth it.

Four valuable resources for me have been *The New Moody Atlas of the Bible*, *Holman Illustrated Bible Dictionary*, *The Ancient World: A Social and Cultural History*, and *The Greco-Roman World*. These will give you a good overview of the land and the culture of the Bible. As you begin to learn more about the culture and context of the biblical writers, you'll discover a depth of clarity you never had before. Some passages that seemed odd become clear. Do the work. Learn and know the historical context.

Leave Your Theological Presuppositions at the Door
Those of us who enjoy theological discussions and theological study have a problem. We typically like systems, and we end up explaining passages of Scripture so that they will fit into our precious system. I love theology. However, I've learned that I must approach theological systems with my eyes wide open and my discerning hat on. Why? Theologians like systems. Sometimes—in our actions and not our intentions—we end up elevating a system above Scripture.

Here's the point: in order to be true to the passage you are reading, you need to read it, hear it, listen to it, consider it, and let it in. This is impossible if your theological presuppositions are on your shoulder arguing with the text. Now, none of us would admit we've ever done this, and maybe you haven't. The truth remains: we have a hard time when passages confront our presuppositions.

If you don't leave your presuppositions at the door, you'll be hindered in understanding what the text is saying. I know such and such verse says this and another verse says that, but what does *this* text say? To be true to exegesis, you need to take in that text alone—at least for a moment. Tell your presuppositions to stay outside for a moment while you honestly consider the text at hand.

Input the Text into the Grand Narrative of Scripture— Preach the Gospel Every Time

Once you've done the hard work of following the author's flow of thought, knowing the historical context, and leaving your presuppositions at the door, you've discovered what the text is saying. Next, and often missed in people's preaching and teaching, you need to input that text into the grand narrative of Scripture. How does this text fit into the whole Bible? How does it ultimately connect to the gospel of Jesus? No matter the text, it has a place within God's overall story of redemption. Your job here is to find out where that place is.

Let's say you're preaching through an epistle of Paul and you are focused on a passage that is calling Christians to live a certain way, you know, be holy and all that. Well, you'd be doing your congregation a disservice—a major one—if you preach the ethics of Christianity without also preaching the life-change of Christianity. How can we live this way? God has given us a gift, a revealed mystery: Christ in us! He enables us to live the way Paul has called us to live. In fact, Paul's flow of thought demonstrates that right behavior flows from Christ's work in us.

Or let's say you're preaching from the Old Testament. Let's say you're preaching on David running from King Saul. You consider how hard it must have been for David to be running from the most powerful man in the nation. You then consider how we have been on the run from sin for all our lives, but we now have a deliverer—Jesus. God delivered David; God will deliver you through Jesus.

6: GET THE RIGHT TOOLS

In this chapter we want to equip you with some valuable tools for your daily sermon preparation. At the outset, let's be clear: tools are only as useful as you make them. You won't find anything in here that will make preparation a breeze, but you will find some things that will aid you and help you remain creative, organized, and efficient. Let's jump in!

A Foundational Tool of Sermon Prep

I have a routine when I am preparing my message for Sunday morning. But something that has immeasurable impact when crafting my sermons is something I do outside of my set sermon prep time.

That "something" is regularly reading.

Now, reading commentaries and the Scriptures I am pulling from for my sermon is a given in rigid prep time, but what I am talking about happens in the morning when I wake up or in the evening right before I go to bed.

Regularly reading helps me produce illustrations, manage content, and grow as a communicator.

I am talking about reading a book (physical copy, e-reader, tablet, phone), and not just preaching books or theology books, but biographies, fiction, historical non-fiction, or anything you are interested in. There is inherent value in that information, whether it sparks a lifelong interest or hands you a story on a platter to share with your congregation.

When you read consistently, you have a wealth of information stored in your brain that can access anytime, and this is a key skill for preparing sermons.

It doesn't end at just reading books, though.

Read the News

Regularly reading local news, national news, and global news can be a big help as well.

A communicator should be relevant, and one way to achieve relevancy is to stay current on the news that is affecting people. The news is, in principle, story, and a good story is always something a communicator needs.

Read Blogs

Another place to read effectively is blogs. Reading what people in your profession, other communicators, storytellers, or people you disagree with is vital in your well roundedness as a communicator. As preachers we have a responsibility to continually and consistently improve at our craft.

Blogs are a good way to filter through other professionals' thoughts and figure out which principles, pieces, and particulars can most benefit you as a communicator.

A good principle to remember is that an isolated communicator is most likely going to be an ineffective communicator.

Stewardship and Reading

One way to branch out effectively as a communicator is to read consistently. Books, newspapers, blogs, anything to stimulate learning and connection to culture within you are effective ways to improve.

Be a good steward of time when reading, reading something worthless or empty can be a huge waste of time. Try to evaluate the best you can whether or not a source is going to be valuable to your mind, work, and communication before you spend hours with it.

Reading consistently from many sources can have a valuable impact on your communication. This is why reading consistently is an underrated and rewarding tool in sermon preparation.

So start reading consistently today!

THREE TOOLS TO GET YOU ORGANIZED AND EFFICIENT

Every single day presents new opportunities for you to add to your illustration, story, joke, and fact library. Every single day you encounter something *that will preach*. But when you find these gems, what do you do?

Many pastors, I'm sure, still use a physical filing system for all of their sermon prep resources. If they find something *that will preach*, they write it down on a notecard and file it away. I have a lot of respect for you if you do this. I believe I have found a better way, though, a way that is much more efficient and allows for much better organization.

Below are three sermon prep tools that you can use to have a more efficient and organized system to your sermon resources.

1. Evernote

Many people have called Evernote their digital brain. I can totally relate to what they mean. Evernote is essentially a note-taking and filing system with many features. The best way to utilize Evernote for sermon preparation is to add notebooks for your different sermon elements and then add notes to each of these elements. For example, set up a notebook titled, "Illustrations." Whenever you come by something that would be a great illustration in a sermon, add it to your Evernote.

Evernote is great because it allows you to add tags to each note so that it can be even more specifically categorized. Maybe you came across an illustration on forgiveness. You add the illustration to your "Illustrations" notebook by adding a note. You can then add "forgiveness" as a tag on that note. So the next time you are looking for an illustration on forgiveness, you simply look that tag up and you will see everything you have related to that tag.

2. Kindle E-Reader

I have a confession. For a long time, I rebelled against owning an e-reader. Since then, I have come around and am finding that I like having my Kindle a ton because of a simple feature that Amazon has incorporated with it. Any highlights I take on my e-books go to a web page where I can access them all.

You can go to the site, grab the quotes from a certain book, and add them to your Evernote account under "quotes." Again, you can utilize relevant tags. This is a phenomenal tool! Imagine being able to have a library of quotes and facts from books you have read, organized by topic. That is exactly what this does!

3. Highlighter

Even if you have an e-reader, it is still nice to have a physical book in your hands. You can utilize Evernote with regular books just like with Kindle books. It just takes some extra work. As you read, highlight things that pop out to you and then, after each chapter, add them to your Evernote account.

More Efficient and Organized

If you decide to migrate your sermon prep system to Evernote, I promise you will not be disappointed. You will find that you are more efficient and organized in your research. It is common to get stuck in your preparation while scouring around the Internet trying to find the perfect story, but you know it can take a long time to find that perfect story, illustration, or video. In the midst of trying to find a story for topic "X," we tend to find great stories for other topics. You don't have to ignore them anymore; you can add them to your Evernote and consider using them later.

7: HOW TO TAKE EVERNOTE TO THE NEXT LEVEL

As one of the major tools you can use for sermon preparation, let's look at Evernote in more depth. Evernote makes work easier, more efficient, and much more organized. It's available across devices, so you always have it with you no matter what you are doing.

How many times have you been doing something totally random and an idea comes to your mind? It's this great illustration related to this Sunday's sermon, or maybe it's related to a sermon that hasn't even been planned yet. What do you do?

Well, if you're anything like me, you either write it down or you forget about it.

Luckily for me, Evernote is always available to write that idea down, take a picture of something that relates, leave a voice memo, or anything else that relates to the idea.

I love Evernote.

Getting started with it, though, may seem kind of daunting.

In this chapter, I want to give you three notebooks

that every pastor needs (that includes you). Plus, I have put together a few template downloads you can plug into your Evernote today and begin using.

Three Evernote Notebooks You Need

Evernote is made up of notebook stacks, notebooks, and notes. Notebook stacks are a grouping of notebooks. Many of the things you'll find below are notebook stacks that have different notebooks within them.

1. Productivity Notebook (Stack)

In any given week you probably have a number of things you need to accomplish. You'll probably have a number of meetings scheduled, a number of projects to complete, and a teaching or two to prepare.

How do you keep track of all this? I do this through Evernote and, specifically, through using my productivity notebook stack. Here's what you'll find in this stack:

1. *Meeting Notes.* Any time I have a meeting, I take notes and plug them into this notebook. Sometimes I use my laptop, sometimes I use my iPad, and sometimes I use a regular notebook. When I use a regular notebook, I take a picture of the page of notes I have created and attach it to my designated note for that meeting. It displays where there would normally be typed text within the note editor. If you want to remember what is said in a meeting, you can use the voice recorder that can be

found within the note editor. When you're done, it will create an .mp3 file that is embedded within the note.
2. *Projects.* I utilize this notebook for large projects I am leading or organizing. I can set reminders for specific projects so that I am on top of deadlines. Right now I am using this for a small book that explains the gospel within a narrative structure that we'll eventually give first-time guests at our church. I have the outline of the book in the project note, and as I come up with illustrations or other ideas, I add them to the note.
3. *Week-to-Week To Do.* I oversee three different areas within The Crossing and contribute a lot toward another main area, then fill in wherever else my help is needed. In order to stay on top of things, I utilize a note for every week of ministry. Every day I have specific tasks that I write down and set out to accomplish. If I have a meeting scheduled, I also add it to my daily task list.

2. Preaching/Teaching Notebook (Stack)

Depending on your context, you may have more or fewer notebooks in this stack than I do.
1. *Teaching.* I oversee Crossing U, which is the elective classes we offer at The Crossing on Sundays. Within this notebook I have our yearly schedule of classes, notes on the classes I teach, and a few other things related to leading this area. For you, this may be your

Sunday School notebook.

2. *Sermons/Sermon Series*. I love Evernote for planning out an entire sermon series. I use a template that allows me to lay out the entire series and add notes for each week in one place.
3. *Ideas*. I'm sure you're always thinking of new sermon series ideas, right? Use this notebook to compile a list of possible sermon series so that way when you begin putting together your plans for next year (or next month if you want to be stressed out), you already have a number of great ideas.

3. Research Notebook (Stack)

One task of any preacher/teacher is to research and compile:

1. Illustrations
2. Articles
3. Statistics
4. Quotes

For me, each of those elements of research are individual notebooks within the research stack. A great tool that helps in this endeavor is the Evernote Web Clipper.

Did you read a great story that would relate to some biblical truth? Did you watch a video that would be perfect for showing a real-life example of some biblical truth? Clip them and add them to your illustrations notebook.

Did you read a great article that you want to save so

you can consult it later? Clip it and add it to your articles notebook.

Find an interesting statistic? Was the census data for your community updated lately? Clip them and add them to your statistics notebook.

Reading a great book where you're highlighting a lot and underlining a lot? Compile those quotes in your quotes notebook. Are you reading on a Kindle now and highlighting a ton? Did you know you could take those highlights and copy and paste them into Evernote?

FREE BONUSES

I hope that this chapter has been helpful to you. In an effort to go above and beyond, we have put together a free download of two things you can use in Evernote that will help you get more productive and more focused on what you are teaching.

Included in this free download are:
1. Sermon Series Overview Template
2. Weekly Productivity Template
3. Bonus: 56 Weeks of Preaching Topics
4. Bonus: Sermon Evaluation Worksheet

All you have to do is go to the link below, fill in your information, and you'll receive these free resources in your inbox right away.

Download them here: http://eepurl.com/bdbGhn

8: SERMON SERIES PLANNING

A sermon series is a number of connected messages around a theme or book of the Bible. A well-planned and well-crafted sermon series can be the game changer in someone's life and in the life of your church. God can use it to show someone the value of giving, serving, or surrendering to Jesus.

Sermon series can be great tools of evangelism, and many churches leverage new series to give their congregants invite cards for an easy on-ramp for their friends, coworkers, and family to visit their church home. There's a lot of potential around doing sermon series well, and that's the key—to do them well. This chapter will help you do just that.

There is a lot of advice out there on sermon series planning. Some people say plan out for the next year. Some people say take it one at a time. Some say do books of the Bible. Some say do topical series. But no matter how you approach planning sermon series, the following will help you out.

Be Contextual

Ministry and preaching are contextual practices. You must not only be aware of your context but also consistently and continually evaluating yourself to make sure you are approaching your contextual situation the best you can. Instead of looking at popular megachurches in your area or that popular preacher five states away and taking their series for your own, speak to the people you preach to, not the people Andy Stanley or Tim Keller preach to.

Now there is nothing wrong with finding inspiration from other communicators (I highly encourage it, actually); just remain anchored by your local context.

Be Timely

I like to plan to speak on issues when they come up. Talk about new beginnings at New Years, for example. Whether it is addressing an event on the calendar or addressing issues taking place in your congregation, community, nation, or world, I challenge you to let your preaching speak to timely subjects.

Be Flexible

Even if you are prepared and planned out for the next year, I challenge you not to let that be 100 percent set in stone. The first two principles—being contextual and timely—mean we have to change things up sometimes. That's okay and encouraged.

Be Biblical

No matter how well your series are planned out, they are going to fall flat and inactive if they are not backed by biblical principles. Our sermon series need to be biblical. And no, that does not mean necessarily going through books of the Bible. Biblical sermon series can very well be topical. And biblical book sermon series can very well be biblical. Just make sure that any series you plan is rooted in Scripture and not your own preconceived notions about something.

Planning sermon series is an important task. As communicators and leaders, doing so gets us on track, organized, and efficient. As you are planning sermon series, keep these three essential principles in mind.

CREATE A COMPELLING SERIES

What made you visit _____ church? *The sermon series interested me, so I decided to come.*

Have you ever encountered someone saying that? Believe it or not, I have, and I'm sure many of you have as well. No matter what some would try to tell you, many people *do* care about what is being preached—especially when it's a compelling sermon series.

Start with the End in Mind

If someone were to be a part of every week of the sermon series you want to create, what would they encounter, what would they learn, what would they be called to do, what kind of change would possibly happen in their life?

Fleshing out these questions will help you create a compelling sermon series that is life-change oriented.

Develop a Compelling Bottom Line for the Entire Series

You'll want to do this for each individual sermon as well, but you'll want to start with a bottom line for the entire series. This takes the whole series and boils it down to a memorable statement. It will take some work and some word crafting, but it's worth it.

Doing this not only helps the congregation in taking the sermon with them throughout the week, but it also helps your creative team in the preparation stage. If you have people who create graphics, intro videos, promotional material, etc., this will help them tremendously in capturing the essence of the series in these different mediums. If you don't have people who are doing these things, it will help you in creating them.

Identify Tension Points for the Entire Series

What are the problems in life, culture, etc. that this series resolves? These are the tension points in your series. When you are able to identify tension points, you create engagement. This is exactly how great stories are created. The book or movie opens with a scene and within five minutes there is a problem presented. You can follow this same thing throughout your series, but you have to identify the tension points first.

Then, like every great story, the tension is resolved, and we preachers do this with the most dependable story—God's story.

Once you've identified the tension points in the series, you can better craft each sermon introduction.

Assume People Know Nothing

I'm sure you have a good gauge as to where your congregation is in terms of biblical literacy and spiritual maturity, but you may be surprised that more people know less than you think. No matter how much we know our people, we don't know those first-time visitors who are hopefully showing up each week.

The norm for today is biblical illiteracy. Research has shown that it is on the rise, and we must be aware of it because it shows where we need to start in our sermons—the ground floor.

Don't assume people know any stories from the Bible. Don't! Please!

Growing up I didn't know the story of David vs. Goliath outside of the reference in sports of an underdog story. Seriously, don't assume people know things in the Bible. Many don't.

So when you are creating your next series, keep in mind that you may need to add an extra week to lay the groundwork for the rest of the series.

Get Ahead

The further ahead you can work, the better. I make it a point to plan a year of sermon series. For all of any given year, I know what is coming. I know the Scripture text for the majority of the year and the basic outline for the rest of the year's series.

Whether or not you plan a year ahead with basic outlines, I believe the best timeframe to be ahead for each sermon series is eight weeks. This will allow your creative team (whoever that may be, maybe you?) time to create promotional material, graphics, etc. I highly recommend you work through this timeframe with a small team of people who meet weekly regarding sermon planning.

Sermon Series Planning Timeframe

Have complete at eight weeks:
1. Title of the series
2. Scripture text for each sermon
3. Goal/desired outcome for series

Have complete at six weeks:
1. Synopsis/summary/elevator pitch for series

Have complete at four weeks:
1. Graphics for series
2. Additional marketing material: videos, blog posts, social media posts
3. Direction and tension for week one sermon

Have complete at three weeks:
1. Bottom line for week one
2. Direction and tension for week two
3. Marketing material
4. Marketing plan

Have complete at two weeks:
1. Promotion of series across channels of communication (execute marketing plan
2. Bottom line for week two
3. Direction and tension for week three

Have complete at one week:
1. Continued promotions/marketing
2. Bottom line for week three
3. Direction and tension for week four
4. Complete week one

9: PLANNING A YEAR OF PREACHING

It's one thing to plan a sermon series; it's a whole other thing to plan a year of preaching. Now, while planning an entire year of preaching may sound a little intimidating at first, it doesn't have to be. In fact, we've found that it is an exciting and meaningful activity as we consider how God is moving in us and in the congregations we serve. If you've never planned a year of preaching, let me give you a few reasons why you should consider doing so.

First, planning a year of preaching allows you to set a strategic direction for your church. Second, being a year ahead helps you know what great quotes, stories, and illustrations to save for the year. If you know what's coming, you'll know what to be looking for. Third, planning a year ahead allows you to maximize each season of ministry.

Before you set out to plan a year of preaching, set aside time to fast and pray. Give God your utmost attention and ask him to guide you in this process (and your team if you have one). Be patient as you seek his will for your church in the next calendar year, and be ready to change what you thought you were going to do.

As you are praying and fasting in anticipation of putting together next year's preaching calendar let the following considerations, guided by prayer, be your starting point in the brainstorming process.

Growth Seasons

Most churches encounter predictable seasons of growth. One growth season typically happens around February and leads up to Easter. Another typical growth season happens as the school year starts up again in the fall. Then another growth season occurs during Thanksgiving and Christmas.

As you consider when these growth seasons specifically happen at your church, you can reference your attendance patterns and then use these times to maximize your efforts in using campaigns or series that engage with people on a level that interests them. These are times to connect people in community and service. We've found that a key characteristic of visitors who become attenders and members is involvement in community groups and/or service.

Question: How can you create on-ramps for people to connect during your growth seasons?

Strategic Direction

What big things are on the horizon at your church? What are some things that consistently need to be addressed? In other words, as you assess the environment of your church, what needs changed? What is the vision for next year? Is your church about to start something brand new? Is it going to take a big leap of faith?

The above questions are intended to get you to think about the strategic direction of your church as you plan out a year of preaching. Is there a way to cast a big vision at the beginning of the year that will set the tone for the year's focus? Absolutely. Maybe you should create a big vision series to begin the year.

Question: How can you strategically cast vision throughout the year to further your church's mission?

Thematic Focus

A couple years ago we went through a series called The Story, a campaign that walked our people through the highlights of Scripture. We did this because we wanted our church to know the story of God and his people. We thought this approach would help a lot of people who have never read the Bible to dive in and give it a shot. And we found that a lot of people did just that.

As you consider your strategic direction, is there a single theme or a couple of themes that you want to keep in your preaching calendar? Maybe you're planning on getting the church focused on its mission of reaching the world with the gospel. A great way to further this with the preaching calendar is to focus on the book of Acts and other passages that talk about the purpose of the church.

Question: How can you further your church's mission by examining a theme or two throughout the year?

Balanced Approach

Depending on your approach, you may be heavy on topical preaching or heavy on expository preaching, but what if you set out to have a balanced approach? What if you did a number of topical *and* expository sermon series?

A balanced approach allows you to identify specific needs your church has and craft a topical series around those things, but it also allows you to walk through a book of the Bible. Both topical and expository approaches have a place in preaching, and I believe there's great benefit to a balanced approach.

Question: How can you balance your preaching approach this coming year?

Be Intentional

Fast, pray, and approach your year of preaching planning in intentionally. Don't just preach on things you *want* to preach on, but consider the situation your church is in. Give attention to each of the above considerations and then be flexible because your plans may have to change.

Section 2: Write For Maximum Impact

10: WHEN YOU'RE NOT FEELING CREATIVE

Writing sermons is a vital part of what a preacher does. Not many good sermons are completely off the cuff. Section 1 outlined some processes and resources to help prepare your preaching, now we want to look at the actual pen-to-paper (or finger-to-keyboard) writing process.

Have you ever had one of those weeks where it's a constant struggle just to come up with a few words to type on the screen? When no illustrations, no stories, no interesting insights are coming to mind? When you just don't feel creative, what should you do?

I've had many of those weeks. It's tough because Sunday is coming whether we are feeling creative or not. Preaching is no easy task, and the work of sermon preparation is difficult even when you *are* feeling creative.

Despite how creative I felt or didn't feel, each week Sunday came and God showed up like he always does. Over these types of weeks, I have learned some things about working through them. I pray that these things will help you when you're in a *creative funk* like I have been so many times before.

Take a Break

Instead of prolonging your frustration, get your mind off of the sermon. How many times have you been doing something totally unrelated to sermon preparation when an idea hits you square in the forehead? It happens to me often. So go for a walk, look out the window, take a ten-minute nap (there's actually a lot of benefit to this), make some coffee. The point is to take a break from your sermon preparation by doing something completely unrelated.

Lay Face Down before the Throne

Weeks when you don't feel particularly creative can be vital to your realizing how much you must depend on God to give you the words to say. Instead of simply bowing your head and praying, lay face down on the floor and be silent. After you are focused on him and only him, ask him for guidance. Ask God to push you out of the way and for him to prepare the sermon. Ask him to work through you. Thank him for his faithfulness. Once you've done this, get back to writing your sermon and see what comes. Be patient and be expectant. He will deliver like he always does. After all, when you *are* feeling creative, it's all him anyway.

Read the Text and Surrounding Context Again

It may take you a few times to read through your passage and its context in order for something to come to mind, but be patient with this. Don't just read your focus passage for the sermon, but read the surrounding context. Think about other texts that connect with the same ideas and read those as well. After you've done this, you should have a few ideas to run with. God's Word is living and active, so be expectant that his Word will speak to you. You've just got to be listening (by reading).

Utilize a Whiteboard
I absolutely love using a whiteboard. Call me a nerd. I don't care. There is something about getting my thoughts on a big board that helps me think. I can work through ideas, questions, and structure much easier when I can write on a whiteboard. Utilizing a whiteboard helps me get my ideas out of my head. If you don't already have a whiteboard, I recommend you get one and try it out.

Answer These Three Questions
(1) What do you want the congregation to know? (2) What do you want the congregation to do? (3) What is one sentence that captures the point of your sermon?

If you spend the time answering these three questions, the rest of the sermon will flow from it. Exegete your focus text for the week. Then take the truth from the text and determine the answers to these three questions. Answering these questions will help you get unstuck and move forward.

In Every Moment

Understand that God is the one who will give you the message that you are to preach. It is not up to you to be creative or insightful. His Word stands on its own. The Spirit is the one who will guide you in the process. He is the one who will give you the words to speak.

You *do* need to put in the hard work while writing your sermon; however, don't ever forget that it is not you writing or delivering the sermon, but it is the Spirit of God. He gets all the credit.

11: TOPICAL PREACHING?

There is a big debate in preaching circles concerning whether expository preaching topical preaching is better. If someone falls in the first camp, they decry the use of topical preaching and say, "It's shallow and results in the preacher forming an opinion first and then going to God's word to find support second." Those in the topical camp say, "Modern audiences just cannot sit through a series on a whole book of the Bible, and they need preaching directly relating to their various life topics."

The thing is neither one of these is *the right* way to preach. In fact, expository preaching can be topical and topical preaching can be expository. I do not believe they have to be put into separate categories.

For instance, right now I am preaching through the book of Proverbs. The great thing about this book is I can preach through Proverbs while addressing some topical life needs in my congregation. This is the best of both worlds.

This chapter will look at how to avoid the dangers of topical preaching; chapter 12 examines the dangers of only doing expository preaching.

The point of expository preaching is to carefully study a text and then bring out the biblical author's original meaning. My question to you is: why can't topical preaching do this? It can if we avoid three things.

Sticking to Our Preconceived Notions No Matter What We Find
If I find a topic I feel I need to address in a sermon, I usually already have an opinion on that topic. This can be dangerous because I can decide on a topic, Google it or look in a concordance or Bible dictionary for the best passage to support my opinion, then build my sermon off of that. I can do all this without any careful exegetical study on the passage I am using.

This could even cause people to throw out a new idea or opinion they "find" in the text merely because they did not want to do the extra work and study.

Repeating the Same Topical Studies Over and Over Again
Unfortunately, I see this often. Preachers like to speak on the same "life topics" over and over again. I get the temptation. But the Bible is broad and addressees many themes, issues, and people. Expand your horizons.

Ignoring the Difficult Parts of the Bible
Many times topical preaching avoids the parts of the Bible that are messy as "life topics." But the Bible is filled with

stories and people that were not perfect. Let's stretch ourselves out and preach these things as well.

Topical preaching is and can be effective. We just have to be careful with it. Now, what about preaching expository sermons? Keep reading!

12: EXPOSITORY PREACHING?

Did you know that there are dangers in whichever preaching approach you take? I'm going to share with you five dangers of expository preaching because both approaches (topical and expository) come with their fair share of cautions and benefits.

No matter what approach you lean toward, I highly recommend you utilize both throughout your preaching calendar.

Leaving the Congregation at the Train Station

Expository preachers tend to leave their congregation at the train station. Think about this: *Good morning. Today we're going to talk about Romans 14:1–7a. Please open your Bible there and we'll get started.*

I don't know about you, but it seems that an introduction like that already has the message leaving the station before the congregation even knows if they want to go along for the ride. I know, they should want to get on board simply because you are preaching God's Word. Oh, how we all wish it were that simple.

But here's the truth: people care about what is helpful and true more than they care about what is only true.

Solution: Answer these questions. What's a problem you are going to help them solve through God's Word? What kind of life experience does the text speak to? How can you create tension with a reality that the text will resolve?

Explaining the Original Language Too Much

If you're like me, you like to geek out on the original language. I get it. I do. But here's the thing: what are you trying to accomplish in bringing it up? I'm not against bringing up Greek or Hebrew in a sermon, but make sure it is moving your congregation toward the goal of the message. By the way, your goal should not be making sure that they simply know what the text says. The goal is for them to *respond* to what the text says.

Solution: Filter your original language use through a filter. Your filter should be the goal of the message. Is this relevant to moving them toward the goal? If not, don't worry about sharing it.

P.S. Most of them don't care . . . I know, tragic!

Stopping the Author in His Tracks

One of my biggest pet peeves is when (a) chapter breaks break the author's thought, or (b) the preacher stops his passage of focus in the middle of the author's thought or argument. As an example, whenever Paul speaks to a church about *living the right way*, he speaks to their reality as people who have been made new in Christ. If this is how Paul argues for morality, we should absolutely argue that very same thing (and yes, in the same sermon!).

Solution: Read the text carefully. Don't pay attention to chapter breaks and section headings. News flash: they are not part of the original manuscripts. They were added! Don't trust them; ignore them. If they end up working well, cool. If not, you'll be glad you ignored them.

Be careful in choosing how you segment the individual sermons in a series that is going through a book of the Bible. Don't just split a chapter in half or just preach chapter by chapter. That might work, but don't automatically do that. Pay attention to the flow of the author's argument and thought.

Keeping Everything Theoretical or Theological

It's easy to spend a ton of time in your sermon to tell people what the text says and to explain how this relates to our understanding of some theological truth. It's also easy to speak in generalities and keep everything theoretical. Again, what is your goal in preaching? Is your goal transformation? If it is, you *have* to apply the text to real-life situations.

Solution: Think about how the passage relates to you personally. If you have a story or two, share them in your message. If you can see a clear application (I hope you can), then make the connection. Never let your congregation walk away wondering, "What should I do because of the message?" Your application of the text should be as clear as your explanation of the text.

Explaining Away the Text to Fit Your Theology
Nothing is worse than a preacher reading a passage of Scripture and then explaining away the tough parts of the passage the rest of the message. Don't let yourself do this. After all, you're not that smart. You need to preach what the text says and apply it to people's lives. Be humble enough to realize that the Bible doesn't care what your theology is. It doesn't care about whether or not you are a Calvinist or an Arminian. It says what it says.

Solution: Preach the Word no matter how uncomfortable it makes you. Stand firm on the Word of God and don't waiver from speaking on the tough issues it addresses. If you stick to preaching the truth of Scripture, people will be offended, but they won't be offended because of some idea you came up with. They'll be offended because the Word of God is sharper than any double-edged sword. It pierces to the depths of the heart. Let it do its job.

A Better Way?
While most people focus on these two main approaches to preaching, we would like to share with you an alternative that we believe is superior to both. That's a bold statement! Keep reading.

13: A BETTER SERMON TYPE

What if expository preaching and topical preaching weren't the only options? What if there was a third option—a better option?

I think there is. I call it exposical preaching. Yes, I know—very creative.

The debate is an interesting one. Some people get passionate about the camp they fall into. Some people *only* preach expository sermons and sermon series. Some people *only* preach topical sermons and sermon series.

Like many things in life, we have a tendency to overreact and watch the pendulum swing in the complete opposite direction rather than finding a happy middle.

My proposal is this: You can be topical when preaching an expository sermon and you can be expository when preaching a topical sermon.

Not only is it possible, but I think it's best.

Imagine taking a topical sermon series and instead of touching on forty different passages or verses in a single sermon, you take one main passage and added one or two supporting passages to the mix. In the same way, when you're preaching through a book of the Bible, instead of settling with preaching through five or ten verses at a time, you preach through the thoughts of the writer. This will naturally point you to a theme, or a *topic*, for that week's message. It should be noted that there are indeed themes and topics addressed in biblical books. They just may not be covered in five to ten verses. You may have to cover a little more.

Exposical preaching takes the best of expository preaching and the best of topical preaching and fuses them together. You'll get the rich analysis of the passage and the rich application of the passage. Sometimes both of these aren't present in the traditional camps of preaching, but they are both vital to and present in exposical preaching.

INGREDIENTS OF AN EXPOSICAL SERMON

An Emphasis on a Single Passage

I strongly believe that the best option for preaching a sermon is to park in a single passage, regardless if you are going through the whole book as a part of a series or not. This may also look like utilizing a couple of consecutive passages in the same book to illustrate the author's thought and then pointing to the topic or theme he is addressing.

There are some situations when you *need* to use more than one passage, such as when you are preaching about the Trinity. You won't find a single verse or passage that teaches this doctrine, but you can teach it by pointing to multiple passages. I would say this is the exception to the rule. An option in this, though, is to do a three-week series on the Trinity and cover God the Father in week one, God the Son in week two, and the Holy Spirit in week three.

An Exposition of What the Text Says

Using a single passage in your sermon gives you the time it takes to expose what the text says to the original audience and then point out what it means today. If you put people in the context of the original audience of the passage, you are helping them truly understand the passage and opening their hearts and minds to its application.

A Heavy Dose of Application

By truly exposing what the text says, you can now turn your attention to helping your church make sense of the passage and apply it to their lives. Spend time addressing what the application of the text looks like for each stage of life and situation that resonate with your congregation. Show them how doing what the Word says will change their lives. Show them how it's vital that they apply this text of Scripture.

Make the application (1) relevant, (2) simple, (3) urgent, and (4) vital.

In Every Sermon

Resolve to stay true to the text of Scripture and apply it to today's times. Preach with passion and energy. Show your congregation how much the text has spoken to you and help them experience that same thing.

It takes hard work to make a sermon rich in both exposition and application, but it can be done. By adopting exposical preaching, you'll be well on your way to doing those two things in every single sermon you preach.

14: BEST PRACTICES FOR OUTLINING

Once you have decided on a series and a passage for a particular week, it is time to outline!

Now, I have heard from a lot of guys, "Ah I don't use an outline; it just gets in the way of me being free up there." I used to say this, too! But I do not think this is a good argument. Unless you are the super, uber, and top-notch public speaker—I am talking MLK/JFK/Abraham Lincoln level, then you probably should have some sort of outline somewhere in the process giving a sermon.

No, I am not saying you have to have the outline up with you on stage. We would actually encourage that you take as little as possible with you up there. But you do need to structure your message. Andy Stanley presents a clear method for outlining sermons in his book *Communicating for a Change*. Stanley refers to it as a map, specifically a road map. How are you going to get from point A to point B and so on?

This is the best way to look at outlining your sermon. Here are a few principles:

Outline with One Main Idea

This is important. Growing up I heard sermon after sermon that took a passage of Scripture, ran with three or four alliterative points, and then concluded. The problem was these often seemed like three or four different sermons.

The easiest way to make sure you are on task is to highlight one main idea or point.

Outline Your Sermon in a Way that is Memorable to You

This is an important aspect of sermon prep in general. If you create an outline or a roadmap that you can mentally recite over and over during the week, then you have a good chance of being able to grow in your delivery. Delivering the sermon note free or increasingly note free is a good goal to have! Creating a memorable outline can help you achieve this goal.

Outline to Introduce Tension and Resolve Tension

When you are outlining, keep tension in mind. Always introduce tension (a problem that needs solving) in your introduction. Think about how you can best keep people's interest through tension as you move from point to point. And make sure this tension is resolved through the structure you have created in the outline.

Try to Incorporate New Structures Weekly
Consistency is good, but also stretch yourself a little. Maybe you like deductive reasoning, so it would be good to outline inductively once in a while.

Create an Outline the Audience Can Follow
This is an important principle. If you do not outline because you want to be "free," and therefore end up scattered, your audience is going to be scattered as well. Have an outline structured well enough outline that you can include guided notes in your program or bulletin, or on the screen if you have that capability.

What Works?
All in all, find what works best for you!

I know outlining can be an evil word to some, but it is an effective tool in your sermon prep and sermon delivery. As you go through your process maybe you figure out outlining is an early part of your prep that you put on paper (or a computer screen), memorize, and go from there. Great! But for most of us I would say the physical outline plays a bigger part in our prep and delivery (even to the point of having it in some form on stage with us), so because of this we have to work to make outlining as effective as we can.

Your outline creates a structure, and structure in preaching is vital.

15: STRUCTURING A STICKY SERMON

If your sermon isn't sticky, it won't stay with those who hear it. If your sermon isn't sticky, it'll bounce off them and be lost forever. A memorable sermon several vital features:
1. It solves a problem.
2. It's true.
3. It's helpful.
4. It's focused.
5. It's action-oriented.

In order to craft a sticky sermon, you have to structure your message in a way that naturally includes these five vital features. The following sermon structure will make your next sermon sticky. It will stick with your congregation because it naturally includes each vital aspect of a sticky sermon.

Engage
Begin your sermon with a story, an interesting fact, a provocative quote. Don't just start your sermon slow;

instead, say something that will hook people, get them to look at you and pay attention to what you're saying. You have a limited time to engage your listeners so that they will stick with you throughout the message. Think long and hard about how you can best gain their attention.

Tension

From engagement, you need to move to tension. Here you're bringing up a problem. If you engage the congregation with something related to life as a single person, you should create tension around being single. It's important to make sure what you say in engage is related to your message as a whole. This will naturally allow you to create tension. The tension you create should make people lean in and give them an opportunity to anticipate the tension's resolution.

This is the time when people realize how your message will help them. An easy way to start is to engage and create tension around felt needs (managing relationships, dealing with pain, finding purpose, eliminating worry, etc.). From there you can move to the next section, which will resolve the tension. It's important to note that you shouldn't resolve the tension so quickly that you lose your audience's attention.

Truth

Once you have engaged the congregation and presented some kind of tension, you can now go to God's Word to resolve that tension. This is where you set the context for the text at hand and walk through the text to teach the congregation what it says. Don't rush through this. Make sure you make God's truth the center of your message.

The following section, application, occurs in conjunction with truth. It should happen naturally as you are teaching through Scripture and come to a point after you teach through Scripture.

Application

In order to know how to apply the text, you need to know what the text meant to its original author and hearers. Once you know that, you can transfer it to today.

Jesus said this → this is what it means → this is what it means for you

As you walk through the text, application will happen naturally. In addition, though, this section is where you can introduce your big idea/bottom line/sticky statement/tweetable statement. If you can't boil your message down to one memorable statement, you're not done with your preparation. People need to take their message home with them. If you can boil it down to one point and wrap that point in a sticky, memorable statement, you are on your way to having a sticky sermon.

Inspiration

This section could as easily be called reflection, depending on what your message is trying to accomplish. Some messages will need inspiration to motivate people to *do something*. Other messages will need reflection to motivate people to *examine themselves*.

This is when you can ask great questions. It's much easier and effective to ask a great question here than it is to say another thing that is true. You've done that already, and if you've done it well you should be able to ask a question that will inspire people or cause them to reflect.

Another way to do this is to say something like:
- Imagine what it would be like if...
- Imagine what your life would be like if...

Engage people's imaginations here. Get them to connect the dots. If you've applied the text well, they will be thinking of something that relates to their life already. Just dig deeper in this section and help them move toward the goal.

Action

I wholeheartedly believe in pointing your sermon to an action step. This could be where you invite people to begin their relationship with Jesus. This could be where you assign them some homework like reading Scripture, praying a prayer, or something outwardly. The action step has no limits. You could use this time to challenge people to join a small group or to serve in a ministry. It could be a time when you point them to give toward some campaign. It could be a time when you tell them to ask themselves a question every day. Again, this section is limitless.

Think through what you want your people to do in light of your message, then spell it out plainly to them.

Messages That Make a Difference

I believe that this way to structure a sermon is highly effective. I believe that if you take time to walk through this structure, your messages will begin to make a difference in people's lives.

By following this structure, you'll naturally include the five vital features to a sticky/memorable sermon:

1. It solves a problem.
2. It's true.
3. It's helpful.
4. It's focused.
5. It's action-oriented.

Imagine what it would be like to hear stories of people taking action in light of the message that you spent so much time working on.

It's time to resolve to no longer have sermons made up of random parts that vaguely point people in a direction. Do the hard work of conforming your message to one idea and one focus. When you do, your messages will make a bigger difference than you can even imagine.

Draw the Boxes

If you don't already have a whiteboard, I highly recommend you get one. It is helpful to draw a box for each part of the sermon and fill in the boxes with an idea or two. If you have to, just use some notebook paper. Once you know the passage of Scripture you are focusing on, you can begin your sermon writing with filling in these boxes. Once you've done that, the actual writing of your sermon should be smooth.

16: REASONS YOU SHOULD MANUSCRIPT YOUR MESSAGE

After you have outlined and created a sticky structure you have decisions to make. Should you write a manuscript for your message? Should you not manuscript your message? If you should, then why? I say you should, and the rest of this chapter is my attempt to tell you why.

Early on I wrote a manuscript for every sermon I preached. Then I abandoned writing a manuscript and began to write my sermons in an extended outline format. Since, though, I have made another tweak back to writing a manuscript for every sermon I preach, and I am so glad I did.

So, whether or not you write a manuscript for your sermon, I'd like to offer you four reasons why you should.

1. Manuscripting Your Message Forces You to Think Through the Specifics
When I prepared my sermons using an extended outline, I left gaps of thought. Even though I did this on purpose, I believe it's vital to know the essence of what you want to

say before you get up on stage in front of the congregation. After all, when God's Word says things like, "Not many of you should become teachers, my brothers, for you know that we who teach will be judged with greater strictness" (Jas 3:1 ESV), I want to be sure that I am going to explain what the text *actually* says.

This is also useful when you think about *how* you want to explain certain ideas. I strive to make every sermon a sticky sermon, and a big part of this is creating a memorable sticky statement that embodies the main point of the message. Manuscripting my sermon causes me to think through the specifics of transitioning into the sticky statement or main idea. I can set it up to have maximum impact in the moment if I do the hard work of writing it all out before I preach.

2. Manuscripting Your Message Allows It to Be Easily Used in Other Formats

In our time of blogs, vlogs, live video broadcasts, online courses, self-published books, YouTube clips, and beyond, it's vital that your sermon is easily re-tooled and re-utilized in other formats. So if you want to make the most of your sermon, then manuscript your message.

One of the extra things we do at The Crossing is *Sermon to Go*, which is a bite-sized PDF summary of the message that we send out to the congregation. It's kind of like a reader's digest of the most recent sermon at the church. The reason I bring this up is that if our team only had my preaching notes (I don't preach from the manuscript, by the way—more on that below), it would be difficult to come up with a good *Sermon to Go*.

I love that at any time I can go back to any of my messages, see exactly what I wrote down to say, and then re-utilize the content for something else that will help people's walk with God.

Ever thought about self-publishing a book? If you preach in sermon series, you have book ideas with a lot of the work already done. You'll want to get permission from your leadership (just in case), but when you have five weeks of manuscripts on the same big idea or book of the Bible, you've got a chunk of a book already done. You'll need to edit it and re-work it for a book, but you'd have to edit for a book any way.

3. Manuscripting Your Message Makes You a Better Writer

I love to write. It's why I have two blogs of my own and why I started our church's blog. I also love preaching and teaching, and one of the things I love about writing a manuscript for my sermons is that it improves my craft as a writer.

Writing something for it to be spoken *is* different than writing something for it to be read, but either way you'll improve in word crafting and begin saying things that pack more punch.

4. Manuscripting Your Message Makes You a Better Preacher

I truly believe this. When you have spent the time crafting the *way* in which you are going to say something, you'll say it with more oomph behind it. If you're married, you know that the *way* in which you say something is just as, if not more, important than *what* you say.

The same could be said for preaching. It's important *what* you say, but the *way* you say it is important as well. Often times the emotion in you is what causes people to connect with you because they can hear the way in which you are saying something is coming from the heart (because it is). When a message pulls at your heartstrings first, others will feel it when you preach it.

Should You Preach from Your Manuscript?

That's completely up to you. I don't. I am working toward minimizing the notes I use when preaching. I have a system for taking the message down from a manuscript to my preaching notes. It's tedious, but it helps me a lot. More on this in the next chapter!

17: HOW TO MOVE FROM MANUSCRIPT TO PREACHING NOTES

I'm a big proponent for writing manuscripts of sermons. However, I'm not a big proponent of preaching from your manuscript. I do admit, however, that many preachers preach from a manuscript and they do it well. Does it work for me? Absolutely not! Instead of preaching from the manuscript that I spent so much time writing, I take extra time and boil it down to what I will take up with me on my iPad mini onto the stage. Here's how.

In order to do this well, you must manuscript your message in a way that anticipates the move you'll need to make. Doing this step well will save you a lot of time. Just for specificity's sake, my manuscripts for a sermon of thirty-five minutes end up being anywhere between 3,000 and 3,500 words. As I move to creating my preaching notes (based on the manuscript), I end up at around 1,200 words or fewer. This final number fluctuates depending on the message. And it's important to note that my goal is to dwindle this down so small to where I eventually have just a notecard with a couple of specific prompts with me.

How to Structure Your Manuscript to Move to Preaching Notes

No matter what writing program you use to write your messages, you must get used to using headings if you want to use this system. In Microsoft Word, you can find various preset headings under the styles menu at the top. If you use Pages, you'll see them at the top right. Every writing program should have preset headings to make your life much easier (as opposed to bolding and increasing font size manually).

Utilizing headings in your manuscript is what will make moving to preaching notes seamless. If you do a good job of outlining your message before you write out your manuscript, you should know what is coming before you write it. This will allow you to label each section with a heading that captures—in as few words as possible—what that section is about. In addition, you'll probably find that each section contains smaller subsections. Label these subsections with smaller headings—you'll be glad you did, I promise.

How to Move Content to Your Preaching Notes

Copy and paste. Done.

Okay, it's not that simple. But then again, it kind of is. *What* you decide to copy and paste is important, though. You'll need both your manuscript document open and your preaching notes document open at the same time, preferably so that you can see both on your screen.

You'll want to begin moving four things over from your manuscript to your preaching notes:
1. Headings
2. Subheadings
3. Transition Statements
4. Main idea and other specific statements

Odds are, if you are just trying this method for the first time, you'll want to add more than just those four things, and that is totally fine.

Color-Code Your Preaching Notes

The notes I preach from are colorful. The color helps me know what's coming before I get there. If you are going to use this system, it is vital to have your own color code. When you use a color code, you'll end up depending on your notes less. It probably seems counterintuitive that the more you format your notes, the less you'll use them, but I've found this to be true.

The colors I use are highlights of the text within my writing program—I don't do this with highlighters after printing the notes. I preach from an iPad mini and don't think highlighting my screen would be helpful. But even if you use paper for your notes, I still advocate for letting Word, Pages, or whatever writing program you use do the highlighting for you.

Here are the three colors I use in my preaching notes:
1. Neon green—stories/illustrations (if I have a story to tell, it is a heading in the manuscript)
2. Light blue—transition statements (going from one heading to another)
3. Bright yellow—main idea

Boil Your Notes Down Smaller and Smaller as You Preach More and More

Less is more when it comes to preaching notes—if you know your sermon and want to be engaging. As you use fewer notes to preach, you'll find that your delivery becomes more natural and more engaging. Make it a point, every time you preach, to stretch yourself and go behind the pulpit with fewer notes.

Now, let's get into the specifics of each part of the sermon!

18: HOW TO CREATE AN ENGAGING INTRODUCTION

In preaching class at Bible college, the importance of introductions and conclusions were instilled in me over and over again. First, engage the listeners with the introduction! And then make sure you close it out with an inspiring conclusion. (I cannot even count how many times I was told to "land the plane.")

As a young preacher (I still am), I did not always get this principle. I always thought "Man, I want to focus on the meat and potatoes of the message." Or "I want to inspire people in the *main part* of the message." Honestly I found introductions boring and uninspired.

So guess what? Because of that my introductions were *boring and uninspired.* I have learned along the way from many people, especially when I watch them, that an engaging introduction is one of the most important aspects of creating a sticky sermon.

There are many ways to craft an engaging introduction. I would encourage you to develop what works best for you. But, I want to provide some principles of introduction crafting that will help you in finding this voice for yourself.

This is an important topic. I can say with conviction that if you have an introduction that misses the mark, the body of your sermon, no matter how great it is, will not reach its full potential. So let's take a look at these principles.

Make it Personal

This is crucial to crafting an introduction that will set up the rest of the message for success. See if the audience can relate to you: maybe share a humorous story about yourself, or a subject you have struggled with, or something your family has dealt with. This creates a rapport with the audience right at the start. "Okay, I understand where he is coming from," or "Oh, wow he deals with that too; I can relate," or "That was a funny story about him and his family." You can build on that rapport.

Communicate the Importance of the Topic

Most of us will do this some way in our preaching. The problem is it is not always done successfully or well. Even if you are holding off on making your main point bit or trying to be inductive in your thought process, it is important to introduce in some way how your topic is timelessly important.

The mistake a lot of people say is, "Well, it is in the Bible. That's all I have to point out to make my case that it is important." And while that might suffice for us and for some of our listeners, many people are going to need some more than that.

We need to introduce why this is an important subject, topic, or problem that needs to be fixed. Introduce some urgency into the problem; maybe introduce the problem but hold off on offering the best solution.

No matter what though, you need to start communicating how or why the subject you picked is timelessly important.

Touch on the Role Your Topic Has in Culture

Building on the last principle, make sure to address the topic's place in current cultural contexts. There often is a pressing cultural need and you know the perfect Bible passage that addresses it.

This is good, but do not end here. Illustrate the role in culture this passage plays and why it does so. Without this step, your sermon may begin a rudderless journey that misses your audience's cultural needs.

Introduce God's Story in a Compelling Way

Let's face it; many people in your audience are just not all that familiar with Scripture. This can be a challenge for you: can you ignite some interest in them in God's Word?

Bring God's Word to life in the introduction. Add some life into the words on the page. Whatever you do, though, emphasize the biblical passage. Do not allow yourself just to tack some Scripture onto the end of your introduction and call it a day.

The introduction is such an important part of your sermon. Work hard at it!

19: IDENTIFY AND EXPOSE THE TENSION

Take any great TV show and you'll see it. No, you'll feel it. You'll feel the tension created within the show, and it will keep you watching. *I've got to know what happens! Friends* is a favorite TV show of my wife and me, and boy do they do a great job at creating tension. An easy tension point in the show is the relationship between Ross and Rachel. Everyone sees that they *should* be an item; however, the show's writers of just won't let it happen. Your greatest desire in watching that show is to see them end up together. Why? Because the writers created massive tension around their relationship.

You can do the same thing with any movie. And you *should* be able to do this with any sermon. Why? Because a sermon is speaking from the grand narrative of Scripture to the grand narrative of life. These two narratives have identifiable tension points.

Most Sermons Fail at This

If we don't intentionally identify and expose the tension in a text and the life situation it speaks to, we'll lose our listeners and the sermon won't take root in their minds, let alone their hearts.

What happens too often is preachers will, maybe intentionally, identify a tension point from the text, but then they will immediately resolve the tension with their grand explanation and application. All the while, they missed a great opportunity to help people realize the necessity for such an explanation and application.

Don't resolve the tension too quickly. Wrestle with the tension so that your listeners will wrestle with it. By the time you resolve the tension with God's word, they should deeply desire to have that tension resolved. But even now it would be too early to resolve the tension. Why? Because while there's tension in the narrative of our lives, there's also tension in the narrative of Scripture.

Even if you take time to identify and expose the tension in life and then go to God's Word to resolve that tension, you missed a vital step: identify and expose the tension in God's Word. How does what you read identify and expose that tension in an even greater way? It does; you just have to see it.

Again, don't resolve the tension too quickly.

Identify the Tension: Seven Common Tension Points We All Face

If you want to preach better, identify the tension in life. What do I mean by that? Take a look at these examples:

1. We hear that God has forgiven us, but we haven't forgiven ourselves.
2. We want to bring glory to God in our job, but we don't know how that looks practically.
3. Scripture says to not worry about tomorrow, but that's all we ever do.
4. We want a great marriage, but no matter how hard we try, we feel like we fail.
5. In comparison to the world, we're among the wealthiest of people, but we feel strapped and broke.
6. God loves me, but I feel abandoned in the midst of this pain and suffering.
7. We hear that God desires us to live in community, but I still feel lonely and isolated.

I could go on and on with identifying tension points in life. The key, though, is identifying the tension point in life in light of what the text is speaking to.

Start with the Text Every Time: Answer These Five Questions

Preach expository sermons or topical sermons. I don't care. I have adopted a way that can use both: exposical sermons (see chapter 13). In this method, I can preach a series that is topical or expository. But once I've identified the actual passage I'll be preaching from, I dive into it. If I use another passage or two, it will be only to emphasize something from the main text. This keeps the message focused and easy to remember and apply.

Once you have the single, main passage identified, read it, study it, and then answer these five questions:

1. What do I or others *believe* that goes against this text?
2. What do I or others *do* that goes against this text?
3. How might some people interpret this text in a way that resolves the tension of application and action?
4. What problem in life does this text address?
5. How do people justify that problem in their lives so they don't have to deal with it?

Expose the Tension: Move Them from Dissonance to Resonance

The goal here is to not only identify the tension, but to expose it for what it is. Take the tension that you identified from the text and speak to that tension as much as you can, relating to as many different stages of life as you can. Give real examples of how you feel this tension in your own life. Tell a story of how someone else feels this tension.

When you go from identifying the tension to exposing the tension, you'll begin to expose the dissonance in people's lives between what they're living and what God is saying. The key is to tune that tension so that people move from dissonance to resonance.

Dissonance occurs where there is disagreement between a musical chord or inconsistency between someone's actions and beliefs. When people are being confronted with tension, they want to resolve it right away. It's why we can and do justify stupid things. Let the dissonance sit there, though.

Resonance occurs where a sound in one instrument is caused by another instrument's sound or where someone sees the truth in the tension—God's word is the answer. Do you see the connection? God's Word goes forth and causes a change or conviction in a person.

God wants to take people from dissonance to resonance. Resonance is where God's Word answers people's questions.

Preach Better: Tension Points Help People See Scripture in Life

When we identify tension points in light of the passage of Scripture at hand, we are connecting it to real life that people are living right now.

Use tension to engage people, but don't stop there. Creating tension around God's Word and around life is connecting God's promises to life.

Show your people that the tension they feel can be resolved only in the truth of God's Word.

Maybe if we do this tension thing better, more people will be driven to read God's Word on their own.

20: TIMELESS TRUTH, TIMELY APPLICATION

Preachers of the gospel have the most timeless truth at our disposal. The fact that Jesus died for the sins of everyone who calls on his name should be central to every message we craft. As long as we stay tied to sound exegesis of the Bible, we have the truth as preachers covered.

So, then, we must connect this timeless truth with our audience. I do not know about you, but when I was being taught how to preach I was told it would probably be best to do this (connect) all at the end. This is, in essence saving all your application for the end to give the audience a burst of truth applicable to their lives to walk out with.

Now, I do not think there is anything inherently wrong with this approach. But I would propose that you do not limit application to just one segment of your message. Go beyond that and sprinkle modern-day application throughout your teaching points.

How Do You Apply the Text?

So how do we apply the text in our sermons? This is the all-important question, right? The goal is to make the text from 2,000 (and more) years ago seem right at home in a modern life. What I do is simple. After I have crafted a main take-home truth and my main subdivisions, I write "APPLY" in each subdivision. Basically my goal is to make sure I provide a nugget of application in every subdivision of my main point.

If my main point is, "Jesus works through everyone who allows him to," and I have a subdivision that is, "Jesus works where you work," I want to show the audience how they can allow Jesus to work at their jobs. Maybe that means living your life above reproach, maybe that is inviting someone to church, maybe that is being open to spiritual conversations; you get the point.

Broad Reaching

Make sure you also color the application so that it is able to hit as many people in the room as possible. So I could color the last point by saying, "Now a lot of you high school students might not have a job, but your job is school and basketball practice and band rehearsal, so that is where you can do these same things in your life," or "Maybe you are a stay-at-home parent, but I am sure you have some places in your life where you are around others; that is when you can do this."

I have found that story is a great way to communicate the timeless application to your audience. Instead of just saying, "Hey guys, go do this action this week," find a story that illustrates a real person overcoming the challenges of doing the action, maybe even failing a few times before finding the victory they were looking for. This communicates real life to your audience, not just a disconnected reality and empty words that will go in one ear and out the other. If you come to a point where you say, "I really need to bump the application of this up a notch," then incorporate a story.

Application is so important to our sermons. I have heard many sermons that had great research, great teaching points, even a great delivery and some cool illustrations, but I walked out wondering what I was actually supposed to do with all that great information. The way we, as preachers, can connect the dots between the ultimate and timeless truth and real life is to provide solid and timely application.

21: TARGET THE HEART

Tears. They were abundant. Not because the message featured some powerful story of someone defying great odds or overcoming a disease, but because the message featured God's Word piercing hearts. Even more, great attention was given to targeting the heart of each person in that room.

Once you've applied the text to people, you must move to inspiration. If this part of the sermon is neglected, you risk creating an environment where people have a lot of head knowledge about the Bible but little conviction from the Bible. It's cliché to say, but true nonetheless, that we all must move head knowledge to our hearts before it will truly make its desired impact.

The Spirit is at Work

We must realize that when we prepare and write a sermon, the Spirit is present with us, guiding us and directing us. We, of course, can choose whether we follow his leading or not, but we need not doubt whether his leading is there. It is. We must also realize that when it comes to people receiving what we have prepared and, the Spirit is the true deliverer of the message.

If you've preached more than a few times, you have certainly experienced someone coming up to you and explaining how the sermon spoke to his or her specific situation. The thing is, that situation had nothing to do with the thrust of the message, but it helped them through it anyway. And that, my friend, is the beauty of God's power working through a fragile vessel like you and me.

What's at Stake
If you had to identify what the true *why* of your application is what would you say it is? When you can identify the *why* of what you are calling people to do with the biblical text, you can tap into an often-neglected muscle.

As preachers who were trained in Bible colleges, seminaries, and Sunday school, we have plenty of tools at our disposal to explain what the text means, but, unfortunately, we didn't spend much time considering what moves people's hearts.

Start with the tension you identified and then resolved with the biblical text. By responding to the message through taking hold of your application, what would people's lives look like? If they were to simply follow God's Word in this area, how could their lives be different? If you started with tension in mind, then what's at stake should be easy to identify.

If This ... Imagine ...

My biggest frustration in school was not knowing how subjects like math and chemistry were relevant to everyday life after school. If I wasn't going to be a mathematician or chemist, how would I use math and chemistry? I wanted to know the "why" behind the "what," and so do the people sitting in the sanctuary on Sunday. Unfortunately, I never received much of the "why" when it came to math and chemistry, and so my interest in those subjects was mild at best.

What if that is how many of the people in churches each Sunday feel as well? That's a problem! But what if you and I could help people see the "why," and by doing so we could help them develop a passion for God's work and God's Word? All we have to do is target the heart. We must take that awesome truth and life-altering application from Scripture and aim it straight at the heart of our listeners.

If you would do this (application), imagine what your life could look like (inspiration)! If you were to begin memorizing Scripture, imagine what it would be like to be able to answer the difficult questions about the Bible and Christianity that your coworkers ask! Imagine answering those questions and seeing your coworkers ask more questions and eventually coming to church with you! Imagine seeing the day when a coworker gives his or her life to Christ and gets baptized—by you!

That progression of thought is legitimate, but it's likely that most people in your congregation wouldn't equate that kind of impact with simply memorizing Scripture. This is why we must move past the "what" and get to the "why," and inspiration is the section to do that.

Questions That Spark
You don't need to focus so much on making a bunch of prescriptive statements when you are targeting the heart. Rather, spend time engaging people's imaginations and asking great questions. When you ask a question, people internalize how they would answer it. They consider what they know and how they feel. And this is exactly what we want to help them do.

What would it be like to be assured of your salvation?

What would it be like to have a marriage that embodies selflessness and love?

What would it be like to leave the old you behind and embrace the new you?

These are all open-ended questions that are designed to help people see the results before they believe or take action. They all are targeted at the heart because they evoke imagination and emotion. The truth is, people make many more emotional decisions than they do logical decisions. Tap into that fact and help people feel the weight of what is at stake.

Inspired People

Inspired people respond. Their hearts are moved and, as a result, they move to action. Apply the text to life, but don't forget to target the heart. Just imagine what a group of passionate people could do for God's kingdom!

Now that you've inspired people to respond, close your sermon powerfully! Let's talk about how to do that in the next chapter.

22: KEYS TO CLOSING YOUR SERMON POWERFULLY

While your introduction is vital to getting people on board to take a journey with you, your conclusion is just as, if not more, important. I'd like to offer several keys to closing your sermon powerfully in hopes that we can all improve in the way we end our sermons.

1. Know What You're Going to Say Before You Say It

One of the biggest mistakes you can make in closing your sermon is to stare at your notes as you attempt to bring everything together. Many communicators would agree that, at a minimum, you should strive to memorize your introduction and your conclusion. Both of these parts of your sermon should be especially engaging and powerful.

If you put the hard work in ahead of time, the closing of your sermon will be powerful. But make no mistake, it takes extra effort to know what you are going to say before you say it if you are not already in the habit of memorizing your message or parts of your message.

When you know what you are going to say before you say it, you can focus on your listeners and not on your notes.

2. Repeat Your Bottom Line/Main Idea

We're big on one point. We believe that boiling down your message to one main idea is vital to preaching engaging sermons. When you do this, you'll want to find different ways to present that main idea. One of the most important times to make sure you say it clearly is as you are closing your sermon.

This speaks to the advantage of a one-point message because as you close your sermon, you only need to present that one, most powerful idea. Instead of reviewing your five points, you can focus on that one idea.

3. Vision Cast About *What Could Be*

Repeat your bottom line, but don't stop there. Get your listeners excited about what their lives could be, or what their community could be, or what this world could be if they grasped ahold of the bottom line you are presenting.

Give some examples of how applying the main truth of your message could impact their lives. Give an example of how it has impacted your own life. Tell a story and engage with people's emotions here.

Give considerable thought as to how you can best paint a picture of *what could be* and explain it in a compelling way. Don't settle with simply summarizing your message, but do the hard work of helping people see and feel the weight of the message.

4. Challenge with Action

In order to close your sermon powerfully, you need to apply the truth of your message practically. I believe that you should challenge your listeners with something specific.

Don't let anyone leave the church wondering what they are supposed to do in response to the sermon. This will make you think hard at what your message's point is. If you can't challenge with action, you aren't done preparing. Get specific.

As you think through your next message, make sure you spend a good deal of time memorizing the closing. Don't neglect the importance of knowing what you are going to say before you say it. An effective way to close your message is through a call to action; let's take an in-depth look at this next!

23: LIFE-CHANGING CALLS TO ACTION

Since the way we end our sermons is vitally important, let's go into more depth on the calls to action we can use to close the message.

When you end your sermon with a specific call to action, you are tapping into what marketers already know. Now, we're not marketers. We're pastors. But we can learn from marketers. They know, for example, in order to increase the odds that someone will take action on a web page (buy something, subscribe to something, click something, etc.), they need to limit the clickable options to one thing—the most important thing.

We can apply this marketing lesson to how we end our sermons. Instead of leaving people saying, "Now what?" or "So what," we can provide them with a simple call to action in light of the message. There are many different types of actions steps you can end your sermon with. I hope what you find below can be a continued reference point as you craft sermons throughout your ministry. Let's dive in.

Salvation

When the gospel is preached, a response is a necessity. People are either going to be cut to the heart or further hardened to the gospel. Some may seem to be non-responsive, but a seed was sown nonetheless.

When you do a salvation action step as the *one* thing you are challenging people to do in light of the sermon, you'll want to end with it. Tell people to come forward and make a decision.

It's a good idea when you do this to have some other people down front to help in case more than one person comes forward. Have the worship team lead the congregation in a responsive, gospel-focused song.

Call people to come to Christ for the first time. Then praise God whether anyone comes or not!

Small Group Sign-Ups

Our discipleship model at The Crossing is focused on getting people in small groups. We believe it's the best vehicle to grow people in their faith. If you have small groups as well, or plan to soon, you'll want to use this action step on a regular basis.

Most topics can relate back to small groups. Sermons that speak to relationships, pain, spiritual disciplines, and so much more can point the congregation to one thing—join a small group and *grow* in this area while creating lasting relationships with others.

LIFE-CHANGING CALLS TO ACTION

To do this right, be sure people know where to get signed up, how to get signed up, and what they're signing up for exactly. Make sure you have a team of people (if you don't have a staff member over this area) who can follow up with the sign-ups throughout the following week.

Call people to join Christ-centered community in the context of a small group. Talk about the impact of your small group, tell stories of other people being in a small group, show a video promo, or even have someone else come up to share their story and have them do the call to action.

If small groups are important in your church, be sure to have it as an action step in your messages on a regular basis.

Serve Sign-Ups

Jesus said the workers are few. Amen?! If you find yourself thinking the same thing in your context, do two things: pray and call people to action. When people begin serving in a ministry in your local church, they begin to take on a sense of ownership, and that's a powerful thing. If you want people to feel a part of what God is doing in the local church, help them get serving in a ministry!

Over the course of a year, you're going to talk about serving a lot! It's kind of a big deal in Scripture.

Don't beg the congregation to serve. *Call them* to serve. You're a spiritual leader, so lead!

Okay, off my soapbox—for now.

To risk coming off as repetitive: to do this right, be sure people know where to get signed up, how to get signed up, and what they're signing up for exactly. Make sure you have a team of people (if you don't have a staff member over this area) who can follow up with the sign-ups throughout the following week.

Call people to join in what God is doing through your local church. Teach them the necessity of serving, and then call them to take action and serve!

If people aren't serving in the local church, call them to take action!

Invite a Friend

If you want your church's culture to be a culture of invitation—where people are regularly inviting friends, family, coworkers, etc.—then you need to talk about it and call people to action.

Some great passages feature someone inviting someone else to go see Jesus. The woman at the well went and invited everyone she could to come and see Jesus. How simple it could be (and powerful) if you called people to take that very same action!

It should be said: make sure you are getting out into the community and inviting people as well.

A great thing to do on a regular basis is to have invite cards made that feature a friendly invitation ("come join us"), service times, location, and the church website address. Keep it simple and make sure it looks good.

Put these invite cards on the chairs (or pews) in the sanctuary so everyone has to interact with them in some way.

At the end of the message, call people to pick up that invite card (if you have some made) and then invite them to pray for one person they can invite to church that following week, then call them to go and do it.

Create a culture of invitation; talk about it a lot and model it yourself.

Membership Class Sign-Up

This is a great action step for messages that focus on the church's mission on this earth. If you have a membership class (or whatever you decide to call it), then talk about it and call people to join in on what God is doing in his local church.

The gates of Hell will not prevail! If that doesn't make you want to jump out of your seat and get excited, I don't know what will.

Help people see the call in Scripture to belong to a local church and then call them to take action and join.

Talk about the part they play in fulfilling God's grand mission here on earth. Talk about what God has done and what God is doing in the life of the local church you serve in.

Spiritual Discipline

Read this in the Bible, pray for this, give to this, fast for this amount of time, get in solitude this day, etc.

Whatever it is, this action step can be a *powerful* force in the life of the local church. What better way to practice unity than to all be focused on one thing, together, for a day or a week?

When this is your action step, make sure that your other communication channels will push this specific action step throughout the week. Email, social media, blog, etc. need to all be focused on this action step to remind people of the call.

At the end of the sermon, explain exactly what you are calling them to do. If you are able to give them something to take with them (Bible verses to read, specific things to pray about, description of what they are giving to, etc.), then that will increase the likelihood that they will, in fact, take action.

Capital Campaign—Above and Beyond Giving

While giving can and should be included in spiritual disciplines, it's also important to identify the action step that coincides with the beginning of a capital campaign, especially if you will have a pledge Sunday *and* a first-fruits Sunday.

Typically, when you go into a capital campaign, you'll spend a lot of time talking about what the church is doing, but you'll spend even more time talking about *why* the church is doing what it. People will connect with the *why*, so talk about it a lot. But at the end of the day, it takes money to expand, build, and grow.

Make sure that when you are beginning a capital campaign that your sermons each have one, specific action step. Don't tell them four things they should do in a week. Keep it to one.

For example, decide what you are going to pledge over the next number of years or decide what you are able to give on the first fruits Sunday. Today's the day to give toward the *why* and the *what*!

If you are working with a capital campaign consultant, they *should* walk you through exactly how to do this and what will be most effective.

Beyond Listening

This is all about getting people to go beyond simply listening to the sermon to responding to it. As we move forward, we should consider how we can help people visualize the truth they are responding to.

24: USING ILLUSTRATIONS

Illustrations are a powerful weapon in a preacher's arsenal. But sometimes we can become too formulaic about the process. We can go, "Okay illustration here, check, illustration here, check," and on and on. Illustrations are how we bridge a teaching point with real life. So breathe life into your illustrations by doing these things:

INCORPORATE STORY

We talk a lot about story in this book because story is so important. As we look at the Bible, we see it is a big story supported by a bunch of other stories. So when we are looking at how to do this we must always:

Add a Personal Touch

This is vitally important in your communication. I have seen so many sermons that had no personal touch whatsoever. These sermons are filled with removed anecdotes about someone else. Add some personal insights, some personal stories, some personal challenges, some personality into your illustrations. Believe me, your audience will appreciate it.

Show Some Humor

I know not everyone believes that you should be telling jokes or sharing humorous stories from the pulpit. But we say you definitely should be. A simple way to add some effectiveness to your message is to add funny illustrations, personal or not. But, try to stay personal; some good old' self-deprecating humor is always good.

Engage Culture

Please avoid rambling on with illustrations that would have spoken well to an audience in New England in 1703 or illustrations that spoke in a great way to the rural church you were in last year but no so much now that you are in an urban context.

Have Fun

This is important. Preaching is something to take seriously, no doubt about that. But try to have some fun. It will loosen you up, as well as your audience. It will also help you connect with your audience. In particular, when we are talking about illustrations, go out on a limb sometimes and stretch yourself—you will enjoy the results.

KEEP GOD'S STORY PRIMARY

A good principle to remember when crafting a sermon and illustrations is that God's story needs to be effectively communicated through your preaching. So how can we do that? You might say "Hey! God's word is enough!" and I would very much agree with that principle. But, there are things we can do as communicators to more effectively impact our audience.

So when you are preparing your sermon this week, think, "How can I more effectively share God's story with my people?" Here are some good principles:

Share God's Story with Passion!

So many times I have seen a preacher start out a message with conviction, build to a profound story, then mumble through a couple verses, then jump back in and speak with conviction again! What's missing here? A passion for the biblical text! You see many people today view the Bible as boring, and not relevant to their lives (and these are people calling themselves Christians), so when we mumble through the text so we can get back to what is exciting and relevant (our words), we are doing a great disservice to people.

Breathe Modern Life into The Bible

Like we just talked about, modern culture downplays the significance of the Bible. There was a time and day when you could share a passage out of Scripture or a story from the Old Testament and 1) people would know the story and 2) they would automatically understand it was important because it is in the Bible. That is not the case anymore.

So what we have to do is breathe modern life into the Bible. This can be doing a simple thing such as upgrading an apostle's dialect to the modern culture. This may seem like a silly, insignificant principle, but it can pay huge dividends with your audience.

Work to Be Creative
Maybe you do not have the talent to write a quick song, rap, or spoken word on the passage or story you are sharing in your sermon, or maybe you do! If you do have the creativity to do something like this, it could work out nicely.

But what can those of us who do not have these creative talents do? Well, we can share media. Maybe you saw a great TV show clip that will nicely illustrate the biblical passage, or maybe a movie clip, or maybe a video on YouTube, or even a new song from popular culture or something along these lines.

Or certainly there is someone in your church who can add a creative touch to the biblical passage, and this could be an effective way to be creative as well.

Make Sure Your Life is Rooted in God's Story
We cannot speak with passion, breathe with a modern flair, inspire creativity, or be clear and moving without personally being rooted in God's story. So what does this mean for you? Are you inspired by God's Word every day? You should be.

As we talk about illustrating our sermons, we need to remember that our ultimate goal is to communicate God's truth to our audience. We need to work hard to do this.

God's story is important, and so is story in general. Next, we will look at some effective things to do with a story in your sermon.

25: WEAVING A SINGLE STORY THROUGHOUT YOUR SERMON

A while ago my wife posted a video on Facebook that got a lot of views. She recorded me telling our two-year old daughter a Bible story. The way she was engaged and listening was adorable. As soon as I would get done with the story, she would ask me to tell her another one.

From a young age, we have all been fascinated with great stories. It's why we read books, watch movies, and watch television shows. We love stories.

In preaching we typically make it a point to include a story or anecdote within our sermons. I'd like to propose to you an idea that will make your message highly engaging and keep people on the edge of their seats. And yes, I do mean that.

I absolutely love being able to park in one passage of Scripture and interact with it. I believe that the most important narrative in your sermon is always Scripture. That should go without saying, but I can only imagine the backlash this chapter could get if I don't make that clear upfront.

My proposal to you is this: instead of using some random anecdote or telling a story in a specific part of your message, choose to weave a single, engaging story throughout your entire message.

A word of caution: if you're not in the habit of looking for and compiling great stories of people having their lives changed by God, this will be significantly more time consuming than your normal sermon preparation.

If you want to engage your congregation in a unique way, couple the biblical text with your single, engaging story.

How to Weave a Single Story throughout Your Sermon

First things first, you need to find a great story that relates to the Scripture you are preaching on. I recommend you find a story that relates to the theme of the text, illustrates the implications of the text, or gives emotion and flesh to the text.

Second, identify the parallel parts of the story and text. Ask yourself, "Are there common breaks in the story where I can switch back and forth between the text and the story?" If you can begin telling the story or begin reading the text and then switch back and forth in a purposeful way, you'll keep people on the edge of their seats as they wait to see what is going to happen in both the story and the text.

Third, tell them both with passion, energy, and emotion.

Why Do This?
People connect with stories. They can see themselves in the narrative, and they will naturally apply the text to their lives.

When people hear about God working in another person's life, their faith becomes even more real to them.

Telling one main story in addition to the biblical text will help you with engaging with your congregation simply because you'll know your material in a better way.

It will force you to try something new. I don't know of many preaching books or courses that will tell you to try something like this, but I believe it will be worthwhile.

An Example
I've done this a few times in the past and it was a blast. To give you an example of how this could work for you, you'll see link to a video below.

The sermon begins at the 26:36 minute mark. Prior to preparing this message, I had received Jeff Goins' book, *The Art of Work*, which contained the story that I used in the message.

To see the example, go here: https://vimeo.com/126797001

Section 3: Deliver Intentionally and Powerfully

26: WHAT TO DO WHEN YOU'RE DONE WRITING YOUR SERMON

Victory! Your sermon is written. Your preaching notes are ready. What now? The secret sauce!

Preach your message to the wall, your dog, a mirror, your spouse (if she wants you to), or a volleyball (Wilson!!). If you don't do this (and you don't have photographic memory), you'll depend on your notes too much during the delivery of your sermon. Some pastors choose to simply read through their message a few times, but we recommend you actually preach the message before you preach it on Sunday.

If you write a manuscript for your message the way we recommend and then boil them down into notes the way we recommend, then you're well on your way to knowing your message and understanding its flow. The headings and subheadings will act as prompts when you are delivering the message to the congregation. But in order to get to that point, you have to do some extra work first.

Step 1

Preach through the manuscript one to three times. Yes, it will feel awkward if you've never done this, but it is effective in getting to know your message before you deliver it.

You'll naturally begin to memorize parts of the message and be familiar with the word-crafted statements you worked so hard on. As you are preaching through the manuscript, pay attention to how you are saying things. Speak naturally, but with inflection on key ideas (more on that later). Think about where pauses would be effective and where other verbal techniques should be used.

Not only are you getting to know the content of your message in this step, but also you are getting to know the most effective way to deliver the content to your congregation. This can become time consuming, but don't neglect it just for that reason. Do your best to work hard in preparation time and writing time to have the time to do this. Your sermons will dramatically improve.

Step 2

Preach through your preaching notes one to three times. The number of times you go through your message here depends entirely on how comfortable you are with those notes. Our goal is never to memorize the whole message word for word, but to understand the flow and to present the content clearly.

After going through your preaching notes once, you may find that you are confident with the material. If that is the case, stop, then visit the message on Sunday morning and skim through your notes to refresh your mind. You'll want to be at the point where you can preach the message without staring at your notes for long periods of time.

Discover Your Routine
Give these two steps a shot for a couple of weeks, then evaluate any changes you believe you need to make. You may find that you don't need to go through your message nearly as many times as we are recommending. And if that's you, that's great!

Make this time—after you're done writing the sermon—personalized to fit you. The key is to work hard here. You'll be tempted to sell yourself short and depend too much on your notes (more on that a little later), but instead just do the work!

27: DO YOU GET NERVOUS BEFORE PREACHING?

All eyes are on you. Staring. Waiting for you to say something. Many people are sweating just thinking about it. It's worse than a horror movie. Speaking in front of people is still one of the most common fears for people. You may not go so far as to say that you are *afraid* to speak in front of people, but it's likely that you do get *nervous* before preaching. Is there any remedy for this? I believe so.

I think it's natural to get butterflies before you preach. But nervous? I don't know that nervousness has to be a part of it. There are some remedies that will help you overcome the nervousness you experience before preaching.

Prepare Well
When you're prepared and you've done the hard work of knowing your material, your level of nervousness should go down. We've talked about the importance of this when talking about connecting with your audience, because if you've done the hard work of preparation, you won't have to focus as much on your notes.

When you are prepared well, you are focused not on your notes, but on the people you are preaching to. As Andy Stanley often reminds us, we should "teach people the Bible" not "teach the Bible to people." What's the difference? The focus of each phrase.

I'm sure you know the feeling of being unprepared. It's stressful. On one hand you're depending on God even more than normal; on the other hand, you're staring at your notes more or getting off track.

Want to get rid of nervousness? It begins with preparing well. Do the work.

Modify Your Focus

When you get nervous before you preach, your focus is on yourself. You're focused on what *you* will say, what people will think of *you*, and whether or not *you* will deliver the goods. It's easy to become nervous and anxious when your focus is all on you. None of us are capable of doing this preaching endeavor. We are jars of clay. We are fragile. We can't do this on our own.

So modify your focus. Instead of focusing on what *you* will say, focus on the people you are about to preach to. Think about their faith (or lack thereof), their circumstances, their struggles, their prayer requests, their families, their friends, the community they (and you) are a part of.

Focus on the unending connections the Word of God will make within the minds and hearts of the hearers in that moment of preaching. God's Word connects to each person's circumstances and speaks to *their* heart. That's the amazing thing about preaching. No matter the specifics, the Word of God connects.

Don't just focus on the people but also focus on the message. Not the specific words or points, but the spirit of the message. What are the implications of the message for the people? What is the burden you have developed for the text and the people?

Get excited. You're about to present God's Word!

Pray Specifically

Before I preach, I pray specifically for the message that God's Word is springing forth within me and will spring forth to the people that day. I ask God to bless his Word and to do what only he can do—cause the seeds to grow.

I pray specifically for the people who will be receiving the Word that morning. I ask God to open their hearts to what he wants them to hear. I ask him to convict them, change them, to bring about a revolution in their hearts.

I pray specifically for myself. I ask God to push me to the side and to take over. I ask him to lead and let me follow. I never want to preach in my own strength, but only in his.

Still Nervous?

What do you think? Do these remedies actually remedy your nervousness? If not, I would encourage you to ask

God to search your heart and to examine it yourself also. What is causing you to get nervous? Again, I'm not simply talking about butterflies, but something more. What are you worried about, exactly? Is it the pure weight of the endeavor of preaching? I get it, I do. But maybe you're depending too much on yourself.

28: ONE POWERFUL CHARACTERISTIC OF GREAT PREACHING

You want to be engaging in your preaching, right? We all do. We all want people to go along the sermon journey with us each time we preach God's word. We already covered how you can use "engage" as a heading in your sermon structure. But the reality is, we can and should be engaging all throughout the message, not just in the beginning.

But how? How can we connect with people on a level that will cause them to stay engaged with the message? I think it's simpler than we may think. So may I ask, do you want to be engaging in your preaching? This one simple tweak will do it. It will make all the difference.

Want people to take notice of you? Someone once said, "Light yourself on fire with passion and people will come from miles to watch you burn."

Exude passion! What do I mean? Well, for starters, do you get *fired up*/excited/pumped up/whatever else you want to call it when it's time to preach and proclaim the very words of God.

Sometimes we preachers need a reminder that we get to proclaim the words of God to people who desperately need to hear those words. It's easy to get distracted and discouraged about people's lack of response and whatever challenges you are leading your church through. But don't ever forget that proclaiming the Word of God to the bride of Christ is an absolute honor and privilege.

Secondly, do you get *fired up* about what God will do in the lives of those who hear his Word? I mean, come on people. *Enough* with the passion-less preaching that plagues America's pulpits. Are *you* even interested in what you are preaching?

It comes down to whether or not you have a deep desire for God's Word to be proclaimed and to see God change lives.

Don't be mistaken, though, God can and will use your preaching whether you are *passionate* or not. He doesn't need you or me, but come on . . . get excited! You get to proclaim and preach the word of God!

Passion Flows from Your Personality
You may be thinking to yourself, "Well that's just not my personality. I'm not the yelling type. I'm not the 'jump up and down' type." Yeah, you're probably right. But here's the thing: exuding passion doesn't necessitate yelling or jumping up and down. It may, but it may not.

Exuding passion for you will flow outwardly through

your personality. This is the beauty of God's design of making us all unique. It's the beauty of arriving to the place where you realize you need to find your voice in preaching. Not Andy Stanley's, Steven Furtick's, Billy Graham's, Craig Groeschel's, or T. D. Jakes's. You *have* to be you. You are fearfully and wonderfully made, so let God use *who you are*, not someone else.

I appreciate what Eric McKiddie has said at *Pastoralized* on this topic.[1] He outlines six ways to preach with passion from Calvin Miller's book, *Preaching: The Art of Narrative Exposition*:

1. Silence
2. Tears
3. Urgency
4. Volume
5. Velocity
6. Poetry

Want to engage in your introduction? Walk up to the front of the stage and remain silent for ten or more seconds. People will be more than engaged, they'll be uncomfortable. Why? It builds anticipation, and what we typically associate anticipation with something important.

---

[1]. Erik McKiddie, "6 Ways to Preach with Passion (Hint: Yelling Isn't One of Them)" *Pastoralized*, February 25, 2013, http://www.pastoralized.com/2013/02/25/6-ways-to-preach-with-passion-hint-yelling-isnt-one-of-them/.

What happens when *you* get excited? What happens when *you* get convicted and passionate about something? Not sure? Ask your spouse if you're married or a close friend if you're not. They'll know.

If you want to engage people with your preaching, channel that emotion into your preaching.

Some Cautions

Please hear me out. I am not advocating yelling the entire time we preach. That's just annoying. Please remember—I can't repeat this enough—exuding passion flows outwardly through your personality. If you're naturally an intense person, then make sure you realize that and also temper down. If you're naturally a mild-mannered person, then make sure you realize that and also temper up.

Passionate preaching has highs *and* lows. And I appreciate Peter Mead's piece on *four problems with passionate preaching* because he sees the tendency for pastors to hear, "be passionate when you preach" and automatically preach with a constant high rather than balancing the highs and lows.[2]

Here's a truth you can keep with you no matter the sermon topic or text: *contrast is key to engagement*.

---

2. Peter Mead, "Four Problems with Passionate Preaching," *Church Leaders*, http://www.churchleaders.com/pastors/preaching-teaching/154755-peter-mead-four-problems-with-passionate-preaching.html.

When you balance the highs with the lows—in tone, pitch, volume, and energy—people take notice. Contrast is key to engagement.

A Final Word
True passion comes from deep within. It doesn't result in a certain type of delivery. It results in a certain type of urgency around God's message to the people of the world.

Exude passion. But remember that passion will manifest itself through your personality, not someone else's.

You get to proclaim God's word. That's something to be excited about!

29: HOW TO GET RID OF FILLER WORDS

I'll be honest, when I began preaching, and public speaking in general, I was bad about using filler words. "Um" and "uh" were my worst ones. My problem is that in my natural communication I am kind of a slow burner. Any time you ask me a question that requires thought, it is going to take you awhile to get to my answer. So to compensate for this I use "uh" and "um" to fill time.

The problem is, I quickly found out this is an absolute no-no for preaching. It is so annoying to be sitting in the audience and hear the speaker use filler words over and over again. Wouldn't you agree?

Like so many of you I took public speaking my first semester in college. I remember, being a preaching student, I was pretty confident in my standing in the class. I got my first speech back and I had been given a B! I was so confused. What do you mean? I then realized I had a major issue: the use of filler words, specifically "uh."

For my next speech I only changed one thing. My professor recommended that I write "don't say UH" at the top of my notes. I did, and I did better. But maybe that was not the best advice for long term improvement

But I have taken several steps since then to improve my public speaking, and specifically my preaching, in this particular area. Here are a few principles I followed to excise filler words from my preaching and public speaking:

Practice

This is the natural remedy for this issue. Do you spend hours on sermon prep only to get up onto the stage and drag down your delivery with filler words? If you do, then find every outlet for public speaking that you can. Two specific ways that I have been able to practice completely separate from preaching are in teaching and podcasting. Both of these avenues require me to think off the top of my head, and continued practice leads to fewer filler words.

Use Natural Space

Work on your natural pauses. It is ok not to string your words together consecutively for your entire presentation. Actually, it is better if you skillfully and professionally incorporate pauses throughout the message.

Don't Think about It

Maybe this is not universal. But, I know the absolute last thing I need to do is think about not saying "uh" when I am actually preaching. It would distract me from everything else I am trying to do. I would not worry about this issue during your live presentation. Instead, use the first two principles to ensure you do not have to address filler words mid-thought in your actual delivery.

Don't Ignore This

Eliminating filler words from your preaching and public speaking is an important task. As much as it would be great to be able to say, "Oh, you know what, I put fifteen hours of study into this so it shouldn't matter." We cannot and should not say this.

30: FOCUS YOUR FOCUS

Every time you walk on stage, you have an opportunity connect with either your congregation or your notes. Which will you choose?

Let's be honest. Public speaking is a much rarer mode of communication than it used to be. People are used to watching screens that have scene changes every few seconds. Just watch a sporting event and see how often the production team switches between camera angles. This isn't just to show how awesome they are and how great all their video angles are, it's to keep you engaged. If you're in a context where there is not a live video feed on screens in your worship center, then you don't have the advantage of this tactic. You've got to do it the old fashioned way.

What's at Stake?
If you don't become intentional about connecting with your congregation, you'll end up leaving them at the train station without ever inviting them to join you on the train. It's not enough to yell "all aboard" because not everyone at the train station is sure they want to get on the train.

This is why it's not enough to just open your message with "Good morning, we're going to open up to the book of Matthew this morning." If that's your approach, don't be surprised when only a third of your congregation is tracking with you by the end of the message.

Making a solid connection with your congregation is vital not only in the first five minutes, but throughout the whole message. You will connect with whatever or whomever you focus on. If your focus is down and on your notes then, you'll do a great job at connecting with your notes. If your focus on the people who sit before you, you'll do a great job at connecting with your congregation.

Last time I checked, your notes don't need to hear the gospel. They don't need to hear about the love and grace of God, but your congregation absolutely does. But how do you do this?

Focus on This

If you want to connect with your congregation, make eye contact with them from the pulpit. When you look someone in the eye, they engage with what you're saying. Don't miss this. It's the difference between making a connection and getting them on the train, or remaining disconnected and leaving them at the train station.

When you resolve to make eye contact with your congregation throughout your whole message, you will keep them engaged.

FOCUS YOUR FOCUS

You can't do this, though, unless you have internalized what God wants to say through you. It takes hard work throughout the week in order to connect with your congregation on Sunday (so do the work that we outlined in the first two sections!). If you get good at following a process, your messages will improve and your congregation will more readily hear what God is saying through you.

Are you willing to do the work to utilize notes as little as possible?

31: MOVE TO MOVE HEARTS

Preaching effectively is so much more than exegeting Scripture, organizing points, and presenting the content that God has guided you in preparing. This is only part of the endeavor of preaching. If you want to preach powerfully, you must engage on a level beyond words. Movement. Yes, movement.

For some, the idea of getting away from the pulpit is quite frightening. I understand if you share that sentiment. For many, the pulpit is the place of comfort, for the pulpit is the place where God's Word is proclaimed. But, let's be honest: the pulpit is not the only place the Word of God is proclaimed. At least I hope it's not.

The pulpit, especially if you have an old-school giant wooden behemoth of a pulpit, is a comfort zone. It's a comfort because it is a barrier between you and the congregation. It allows you to be separate from the rest of the congregation, and this is a positive thing in the minds of many.

We at *Rookie Preacher*, though, are not about doing things because they are comfortable. We want to grow in our preaching and leadership, and the only way growth happens (you know this to be true) is through stepping outside of your comfort zone. And since you are reading this, we trust that you share that same attitude.

So, if you are afraid of leaving the pulpit, your first step in improving your sermon delivery is to just walk away!

Reasons to Move

Movement engages. Our eyes are naturally drawn toward movement. If this is true, then why do so many preachers stand still when they preach?

Movement speaks. Depending on what type of movement you use in a given moment, you are saying something beyond the words you are speaking.

Movement stirs. The way you move can stir certain emotions that you are trying to express. Slouching stirs discouragement. Jumping stirs excitement. You get the idea.

Movement narrates. A way to bring narrative to life is to change your position when you change characters. Utilizing movement allows you to be multiple characters within a narrative section of Scripture.

Movement emphasizes. Want a way to bring home the point of your message? A certain movement prepares people for the important thing that is to come.

Want some practical ways to utilize movement in your next sermon? Keep on reading.

Practical Ways of Using Movement

To drive home the main point . . . Move forward, toward the congregation. The most powerful position on a stage is front and center. Don't park here for your whole message or overuse moving to this space, but use it when you want to drive home your main point. People know that when you move to that spot, you are commanding their full attention and what is going to be said is of great importance.

To transition into a story, take a step back. This will let the congregation know that you are ending the thought you were in and you are transitioning to something else.

To emphasize opposing ideas, begin presenting one idea while walking to one side of the stage. Once you are finished presenting that idea, begin presenting the opposing idea while walking to the other side of the stage. Whenever you refer to one of the ideas, return to that spot on the stage.

To connect with the whole congregation, make eye contact with the whole room and make *movement contact* (that's an interesting way to put it, I know) with the whole room. What I mean is, don't just move your eyes and head to connect with everyone, but also move toward different spots of the room while you are on the stage. Depending how large your sanctuary (or worship center or whatever you call it) is, you may do this much more or much less than others. The idea remains: if there are four sections of seating in the room, make sure to connect with each by making eye contact and moving toward each section (right to left, not necessarily front of stage or back).

Don't Be Distracting
A quick word of caution: movement can become a distraction. If you have a tendency to bob back and forth when you are speaking, this movement can become rather distracting and retract from the message you are preaching. If you are blessed with having the ability to have your message recorded with video, you'll be able to identify any distracting movements. If you do not have that option, ask someone to tell you if you have any distracting movements.

Be Intentional
To be clear: I am not advocating for movement for the sake of movement. I am advocating movement for the sake of better engagement and improved preaching. Don't just walk around aimlessly as you preach, but be intentional with the way you move while you preach.

Don't be a robot. Be natural, but be intentional.

32: CAPTURE THE EMOTION OF THE TEXT

Emotions are powerful. They can bring people closer together or divide them to the point of war. Emotions. Do you notice them in Scripture? They are there and ready to be captured. But they must be caught. They won't just happen without deep preparation and intentional delivery. Your congregation must see them through you. Otherwise, most of them will miss it. And if they miss the emotion of the text, it may be the difference between a message that touches hearts and one that just scratches the surface.

Now, before I get crucified for making such a claim, allow me to be clear: The Holy Spirit convicts and moves hearts. However, he uses real people like you and me to be his mouthpiece. As we are guided and moved by the Spirit, we must see that we are tools—instruments of communication. We can be sharp tools or dull ones. Last time I checked, sharper is better.

Capture It!

Many passages are bursting at the seams with emotion. Take any narrative in Scripture and you'll be able to identify the emotions that people were experiencing.

Think about when Jesus heard about Lazarus and how he wept when he was confronted with the reality that his good friend was dead. Was he overwhelmed with tears because he was dead or that he was going to resurrect him and take him away from paradise? We don't know. But what we do know is that Jesus has his emotions on full display in this passage.

Consider the man whom the apostles healed at the gate of the Temple. What did he do? He got up, danced, leapt for joy, and praised God. He experienced a joy and happiness that was powerful and meaningful. Everything he knew about himself, his entire identity and self-worth was changed. He now could do what he never could do before. That is powerful!

Emotion is even packed in the Epistles. You can gather the high emotions that Paul wrote with as well as the emotions of his readers. The church in Corinth was facing strife, gossip, dissension, and severe sexual sin from one of their own. They were likely confused, frustrated, and overwhelmed with worry because of what their own gathering had become. Why else would they have asked Paul so many questions? They were struggling!

We could go on and on identifying emotion-packed passages of Scripture. Instead of focusing there this entire chapter, let us consider how we can go about capturing that emotion and then helping our congregations feel it through our sermons.

As you have gathered, you must first identify the emotion in the text. It's important to note, also, that the emotions may not always be this clear. The text may not make clear what the people are feeling, but I believe this is an area where you can put yourself in the situation and consider what you would have been thinking. As long as you don't stray people away from the main point of the text, it's okay to add some color to the situation as you bring it to life before people's eyes.

Second, you must take that emotion and embed it within your own heart as you deliver the message you have prepared. If you've prepared well, you will have already interacted with the text enough to where you are *feeling* it as you read it and preach it.

In order to deliver that embedded emotion, you must help people do two things that will lead to a third: (1) help them *see the emotion*, and (2) help them *hear the emotion*. When you do these two things effectively, the congregation will (3) *feel the emotion* you are capturing from the text.

People see the emotion by seeing it in you. This is surely easier for some to do than others, but if you have spent enough time in the text, you should be well on your way to showing the emotion of the text with your facial expressions, gestures, and movements. If you're at a place in the passage where something sad has happened, don't keep smiling. Instead, droop the shoulders, look down, and move slowly. If you're at a place in the passage where something exciting has happened, don't look so serious. Instead, stand up straight, look out and up, jump up and down, and move quickly.

People hear the emotion by hearing it in you. If you're preaching on a passage that embodies frustration, embody that as you take on the persona of the person who is frustrated. Explain why they are frustrated. Say it in a frustrated way. If you're preaching on a passage that is filled with amazement and wonder, allow your voice to be airy as you consider the object of amazement and wonder.

Observe to Rightly Capture

A practical exercise you can do if this concept is a little baffling is to observe other people as they show and speak with emotion. Notice how *you* modify your voice and facial expressions when you are speaking with emotion.

For a quick insight, ask your spouse how you do this when you are dealing with emotions of any kind. I'm sure she can give you some insight.

Don't Miss the Point

It's easy to read all of this and think that you're getting tips on acting instead of tips on preaching. If this is what you're thinking, I get it! But don't miss this: if we are going to truly help people interact with Scripture, we must interact with it fully ourselves. We were created with emotions. We are emotional. And that's okay. In fact, Scripture is filled with emotions. And this is what I've observed: when people *feel* the message in the text, they are more likely to *respond* to the text.

Now we are going to get into the more technical aspects of delivery.

33: YOUR VOCAL TOOLBOX

"It's not what you said, it's how you said it," is a statement I've heard from my wife many times. *How* you say something is just as important (sometimes even more important) as *what* you say. This is true in relationships and it is certainly true in preaching. The good thing is, you have a choice as to whether or not you will be intentional with not just *what* you say but also with *how* you say it.

Your voice is a powerful tool. The spoken word has started wars and ended wars. It has brought peace to chaotic situations and it has brought chaos to peaceful situations. Faith comes from *hearing*, so we must speak. Your vocal toolbox is already filled with every tool you need. The key is discovering how to use these tools. So let's jump in!

Pitch
Did you know that news broadcasters are typically trained to lower their pitch at the end of their sentences? The reason for this is we associate this type of speaking with someone who has confidence and authority. We take what they say more seriously than we would if their voices went

higher in pitch as they ended their statement. Inflecting pitch upward brings to mind that the speaker has doubts about what they are saying.

Now, don't take that as grounds for turning on your "preacher voice" for the entire sermon. Don't just lower your voice for the sake of lowering it. Be intentional and mix it up based on the context. You likely already do this. When you get particularly passionate about something in a sermon, your pitch rises and your voice gets higher. This is natural and good! Be natural and be intentional.

Quick tips: (1) Use *your* voice range, not someone else's, (2) lower your pitch when making an important point, and (3) mix it up; don't go monotone!

Volume

As you'll discover, these tools are to be used in conjunction with one another. Many people, when trying to get the attention of a room, feel the need to raise the volume of their voice above everyone else. This can be effective; however, the pendulum swing in the other direction is effective (maybe even more) as well.

Go to a coffee shop and keep your headphones in your bag. You'll hear the varied volume that accompanies each person's voice. Some people are loud and some are soft. But then you'll notice that depending on what is being said, the volume of the person speaking changes. You do the same thing in regular conversations, and it's powerful to do so when preaching a sermon.

You can be in a room filled with a group of friends where multiple conversations are taking place and then, without a doubt, someone begins to whisper something to another person, and what does everyone do? They begin to subtly lean in. They do so because whispering (lowering of vocal volume) embodies importance. The same happens when one person raises their voice to someone else. Everyone alters his or her attention toward the anomaly of noise.

Mix up the volume of your voice when you preach.

Quick tips: (1) Try whispering a key point and watch people lean in, (2) raise your volume when you are particularly passionate about something, (3) mix it up!

Tempo

Talk fast and you'll sound nervous. Talk slowly and you'll sound boring. Talk pretty fast and you'll sound confident. Talk slower than normal and you'll sound friendly.

Tempo is powerful. Get the right quick tempo with a string of energetic statements and you'll energize your listeners. They'll get excited and you may even get an "amen." But what's happening is they engage with what you are saying because they have to pay special attention to what you are saying because your tempo is faster than normal. The same is true if you slow down some. People will lean in because they are anticipating and waiting for your next word.

As with all these tools, balance is key.

Quick tips: (1) Use a quicker tempo to bring energy to a story or point, (2) Use a slower tempo to create a rapport with the congregation, (3) mix it up!

Silence

The powerful dramatic pause! There's nothing like starting your sermon with ten seconds of silence. People will be completely engaged with you and nervous for you (fearing you forgot what you were going to say). Silence exhibits authority and confidence. In negotiations, business people know the first person to talk is going to end up losing. Silence is absolutely powerful.

When should you use it, though? A good place to start is when you want to give people space to consider and reflect on what was just said. Silence emphasizes what preceded it.

Quick tips: (1) Use silence right after your main point, (2) use silence after saying something particularly shocking or uncomfortable, (3) use silence after asking a reflective question, (4) use silence sparingly so it doesn't lose its affect.

Use Your Toolbox

Use these tools together to deliver powerful sermons. Pay attention to how you are saying the things you are saying. Be intentional!

34: REPETITION AND EMPHASIS

"You're repeating yourself." When we hear this phrase in conversation or debate it is usually not good, but in preaching it can be used to great effect. Repetition should be used in a macro sense. Make sure you are repeating your main truth throughout the message. You do not need to quote it word for word throughout, but try to articulate the spirit of it in different ways at different times. When we reintroduce our main truth throughout the sermon, we are allowing the audience to see the truth more than once and framed in more than one way. It also allows us a chance to focus and remember our laser sharp truth that we are building.

Using pitch, volume, tempo, and silence, as we just addressed, are great ways to emphasize certain parts of your message, but repetition can be used with just as great of an effect. Repetition can create emphasis. Sometimes I will say something that is important, pause, say, "Did you get that?" and repeat what I just said. This emphasizes what I just said. The audience will realize, "Okay, he wanted us to know that." It also allows the audience a chance to reengage with you.

Repetition is also a way to make your sermon more of an art form. Now, we do not necessarily want our sermons to read like poetry, but repetition is an important part of literary works. With effective use of repetition, you can develop a realistic sense that you are building to something. You can do it like this: "This is so important; did you hear what it was? Now do *this* with that knowledge." For instance, you could say, "God loves you so much. Did you hear that? God loves you so much." Now since you have built that as an important statement, deliver the punch, "So love other people." This is an effective way to build emphasis through repetition.

You can use repetition to emphasize your main point throughout your message. You can use repetition to emphasize the importance of an isolated point you just made. You can use repetition to build to something drastically important and profound. I like to use this rule of thumb: I would rather say something one too many times than say something once short of making an impact in someone's life. Can someone benefit from hearing that again? Okay, then maybe you can make an effective use of repetition there.

We fear repeating ourselves sometimes. "Did I just say that?" might be going through the back of your head, but repetition can be an important and powerful tool at your disposal. I know in conversation I have a fear of repeating myself, but when it comes to delivering sermons, use the function of repetition to your advantage; do not hide from it.

35: WHAT YOU NEED TO KNOW ABOUT USING MEDIA

There are a lot of people who would flat out say they are against using modern media in their sermon delivery. Common objections are that it is distracting, irreverent, or takes away from God's Word. Now, these objections have a bit of truth to them. If we are going to use modern media in our sermons, then we should do so carefully.

Most of us have some kind of ability to use modern media (video, audio, Internet content, etc.) in our sermons. If you have a screen to project onto, then you can do this. (Even if you do not have a screen you can always use audio instead.) Modern audiences are used to phone screens, TV screens, computer screens, iPad screens, and on and on. So we are going to look at some principles for using modern media in sermon delivery. I want to move past just slides on PowerPoint (those are great and highly recommended) to look at using video, audio, the Internet, and so on in our sermons.

Make Sure You Are Legal

This is important because, say, you want to show a clip of a movie you just bought and love so much. Well you cannot project that on the screen to everyone in your audience without permission. A CVLI license is a good resource to have. But if it is not covered you might have to plan ahead and contact the studio to receive permission (you might not get it).

Always Relate to Most of Your Audience

Most video will keep people engaged just by the fact that it is visual and on the big screen and a break from you (just kidding; maybe). But I have seen a whole four-minute song played in a sermon that just did not do much for a large part of the audience.

If you are going to use audio, make sure it is short and will communicate to most of your audience.

Be Aware That the Media is Supplementary and Secondary to the Text

The five-minute movie clip you play at the beginning of your sermon could be a great resource or illustration to help explain and apply the text you are using. But, do not make it the centerpiece of your message. The biblical text, the Scripture, the gospel need to be the centerpiece of your message, and as great as modern media, movies, and video clips can be, they do not have the saving power of Jesus.

Do It with Excellence and Professionalism

This is so important! I have seen so many times when the preacher has a video clip in the middle of his sermon, and when he gets to it the computer operator is pulling things across the screen and minimizing programs and maximizing programs and so on.

It is important that if you are going to add media to your sermon delivery that you do it with excellence. If that means you have to spend some time learning how to do it yourself and then training people to do it with excellence, then do that.

Modern media can play a significant role in the modern sermon.

Section 4: Beyond Sunday

36: EVALUATE YOUR LAST SERMON

One of the main things you need to do after you preach on Sunday is take a look in the mirror. Do you go evaluate your last sermon? Sports players watch film. Musicians listen to their performance. Business people evaluate what happened in meetings. Other public speakers evaluate their talks. So, do you go about evaluating your last sermon? I hope you do.

As people who proclaim the most important truth to mankind, we better do our best at communicating that message as clearly and compellingly as we can, understanding that God's Sprit is at work in and through us. If you're like me, though, you go about evaluating your last sermon and then find yourself simply watching or listening to your message without actually *evaluating* it. You naturally notice little quirks here and there, but you don't make the most out of the process. In hopes of changing that, here are some questions for when you are evaluating your last sermon.

Was What I Proclaimed True?

Let's get an easy one out of the way. Did you say anything off the cuff that was completely wrong? Did you misquote a statistic? Did you clearly proclaim truth within your message?

If yes, then how? If no, then how? It's important to go deeper than a *yes* or *no*.

Did I Build Tension Then Resolve It?

Before you even got into the text, did you engage people and bring tension into the conversation? In other words, did you build anticipation toward a problem and get people on board with where the message is going? Did you get them nodding yes with you, and then did you build in some kind of conflict?

If yes, then how? If no, then how?

Was My Biblical Exegesis Accurate and True to the Text?

Did your hard work of sermon preparation pan out into a clear and concise exegesis of the text you preached on? Did you engage with the text on the contextual level, the contemporary level, *and* the grand narrative-of-Scripture level? In other words, did you place people in the time of when the text was written, did you place the text in the here and now, and did you show your hearers where this passage fits into the grand gospel narrative of Scripture?

If yes, then how? If no, then how?

Did I Engage the Intellect?

Did your *deep study* of the text come through your message to engage people's intellect? Did you make people think about the claims of Scripture? Did you appear as though you didn't half-heartedly walk up to the pulpit with a vague idea of what you wanted to say? Did you *show* people how Scripture results into a cohesive worldview, and did you present it in a cohesive way?

If yes, then how? If no, then how?

Did I Engage the Emotions?

Did your understanding of what people are going through come through your message? Were you able to get beneath the surface to engage people's deepest fears? Were you able to preach to the heart so that people were convicted and felt the weight of the message? Did you display the emotion of the text? Did you use any stories that brought out the real struggle that the text addresses?

If yes, then how? If no, then how?

Did I Connect the Text to Everyday Life?

Throughout your message, did you go from the contextual level to the contemporary level? Did you *show* the congregation how this works out on Monday when they're at work and having a difficult day? Did you connect the principles found in the text to our outward call to make disciples, love God, and love people?

If yes, then how? If no, then how?

Did the Congregation Know What to Do in Response?

Every message needs a response of some kind. Did you call the congregation to do something in response to the message presented? Did you have an action step? Did you connect the text to today to the point of giving them one, specific thing to do? You may think that this is a bit too much spoon feeding, but I've found that when people start responding to sermons with action, they serve more, give more, and come back more. Who would have thought?!

If yes, then how? If no, then how?

Be Honest and Gracious with Yourself

Don't be extremely tough on yourself and don't sugar coat the truth. The only way you'll continue to improve is if you evaluate and make tweaks.

If you want to take this to the next level, give these questions to someone you trust and ask them to evaluate a sermon of yours.

37: HOW TO TAKE YOUR SERMON PAST SUNDAY

With the expansion of technology, you have an extraordinary opportunity to further your sermon content beyond Sunday morning. The thought process used to be (and still is in some places), preach one message on Sunday morning, a different on Sunday night, and yet another one on Wednesday night. The people who came to all three were the spiritual people of your congregation. But times have changed and thought processes have changed.

Is it good to end up preaching three different sermons every week, or is it better to hone in on one message and have everything throughout the week point people back to that one thing?

I think the latter.

Instead of letting your sermon content be forgotten as the week goes on (people do forget your message, by the way), you can do these four things to take your sermon past Sunday.

Sermon-Based Small Groups

Instead of always having your small group content be unrelated to the message—like the old Wednesday night Bible studies—focus them on the sermon from Sunday. Some churches do this all the time and some do this for major sermon series.

There is an art to doing this because you don't want it to simply be a rehashing of the sermon. You want the questions to focus on the application of the material that was presented on Sunday. Imagine if your congregation was confronted with the call to action of your message in a more intimate environment where they had people who would hold them accountable. That is the benefit of utilizing sermon based small groups.

Mid-Week Blog Post

As you were preparing your message, you probably came across things in your study that you didn't include in your sermon. What if you could use that material to further your message throughout the week? I believe you can. If you have a blog or your church's website has blog capabilities, you can put your unused material to work.

If you shared two stories in your original message but had a couple more that you decided not to use, you could craft your blog post around one of those unused stories.

It's important—just like with sermon-based small groups—that you don't just rehash your sermon content.

Come up with a new way to get to your bottom line. Use a different story to illustrate the need for everyone to apply that truth to their lives.

If you don't feel comfortable writing out an article, do a video blog–a short video where you share the same content as you would a blog post.

If you decide to do this in written form, have someone else look over your article and make grammatical edits where needed. One thing is for sure: writing a sermon and writing an article are two very different things. With writing a sermon, you're not at all concerned about grammar because you are writing to speak it. In an article, you're surely concerned about grammar because you are writing to be read.

Social Media Posts

If you are utilizing a one-point sermon, your bottom line should be something that can be utilized as a tweet on Twitter. Various quotes from your message can be turned into picture quotes that can be utilized on channels like Instagram, Twitter, and Facebook. Video clips from your sermon can be specially edited for social media use.

Don't be afraid to utilize hashtags for your sermon or sermon series. Encourage your congregation to engage with you on social media and to utilize those designated hashtags.

Write a Book

While this isn't for everyone and it wouldn't be something that could be done for each sermon or sermon series, this is a no-brainer as far as extending your content not only through the week but for much longer. If you have a particular sermon series that you are extremely passionate about, utilize each week of the series as a chapter in a book to expand on the topic even more than what is discussed in your sermons.

Final Thought

A lot of time is spent on preparing, writing, and delivering your sermon. If you're not intentional about furthering that content past Sunday, you're doing a disservice to the people whom God has entrusted you to serve. God's grace shown through your sermon is important enough that it should be reminding people of its truth all throughout the week. Don't miss out on furthering your sermon content throughout the week.

38: HOW TO HANDLE BAD SERMON CRITICISM

No matter the role you are leading in you are going to face criticism. Some criticism is good-it is constructive, truthful, and has good intentions. Relish this kind of criticism in your ministry. Some criticism is unequivocally bad criticism. It is destructive, not based 100 percent in truth, and is based in bad intentions. Prepare yourself for this kind of criticism. Whether it is a critique of your sermon five minutes after you preached it or a critique of an event five minutes after you led it or a personal attack on you, your family, or your church, this criticism can pull us into the depths of despair. But there are positive ways we can respond to negative criticism. I believe responding in these ways can help anyone relieve the burden caused by unwanted and bad criticism as well as help and minister to those who are broken and dishing out this bad criticism.

Here are three positive ways to respond to negative criticism:

Find the Hidden Truth

This is a difficult task, but much criticism, yes even destructive criticism, can be traced to a constructive or truthful nugget of information. Maybe the criticism was "Pastor, your sermon would have been so much better if it was fifteen minutes shorter." Now, there is nothing constructive about this criticism five minutes after you preached the sermon, but maybe the nugget of truth is you need to find a way to cut some fluff from your sermon.

Find the Broken Person

A lot of destructive criticism comes from a broken and toxic person. Maybe they are broken because they are toxic, or maybe they are toxic because they are broken. Either way, extend grace.

Defend Yourself . . . Kindly

Maybe you casually brush off bad criticism and never confront those who give it to you. This might not be the best path to take. Obviously, a shouting match or heated discussion in the foyer right after service might not be the best place to defend yourself. But maybe offer to take the person to lunch or offer them thirty minutes on Tuesday to discuss their criticism, why it hurts, and why it is unnecessary.

Bad criticism is something none of us want. It is frustrating, disheartening, and discouraging. But in the bad criticism we can find a way to help ourselves and help the person giving the bad criticism.

39: FELLOWSHIP WITH AREA PREACHERS

I know in ministry it's easy to be scared or jealous of the church down the street. Maybe they're growing faster than your church; maybe recently some of your members have gone there. Or maybe there is no reason at all. This is a natural inclination for most of us. We believe in the church we lead, the mission, the exact theology, and everything else about it. We want to see people meet Jesus and grow in *our doors*. But we need to grow past this.

We need to grow past our fear or jealously of other churches and fellowship with area pastors. No, I am not talking about fellowshipping with pastors hours away or your friends from seminary (great things to do by the way), but pastors of churches in your town, city, or community. So here are some concrete reasons why you need to fellowship with area preachers:

Collaboration

Collaboration is a major asset that can come out of getting together with area pastors. What your church can do by itself is great, but just think how much the church could impact the community when individual churches team up and put all they have together and go for it. One church I was at was blessed to have a youth program collaboration in place. In that context, three churches came together and did youth events. This is a great example of how to collaborate well together, but this will never happen if you do not fellowship with other area pastors.

Encouragement
Sure, you can get encouragement from pastors and colleagues around your nation and the world. But no one can give you the contextually specific encouragement. Whether it is a huge problem that your specific community is involved with or a recent tragedy that happened in the community, area pastors can better encourage and show empathy than those far removed from the situation

Community
You can make "doing church" a community effort. Past collaborating on events, you can do an Easter service together or a summer service in the park. One such effort I saw was in my hometown where a bunch of churches got together and did a sermon series on what it means to be a neighbor. Efforts like this can do great work in your specific context and would not be possible without the fellowship of local pastors.

Jesus Wants It

Jesus wants us to work together, not apart, to reach the lost. This is stating the obvious. We should fellowship with area pastors if for no other reason than to please Jesus.

CONCLUSION

We hope that you found many useful insights within this book. We hope that as you walked through each chapter you were given a new tool to add to your repertoire as you preach God's good news.

Let's not end this conversation here, though. We want to invite you to join us as we continue to talk about the practical aspects of preaching (and leadership) on *RookiePreacher.com*, our online resource where we help pastors preach and lead better.

If you decide to join the community and subscribe, we have some great free resources for you.

Blessings to you as you continue in the faithful journey of pastoring and preaching!

Made in United States
Orlando, FL
08 March 2024